OCR
GCSE
(9–1)

PE
Second Edition

JOHN HONEYBOURNE

An OCR endorsed textbook

The Publishers would like to thank the following for permission to reproduce copyright material.

Photo credits:

Page 1© FR Sport Photography/Alamy Stock Photo; **page 4** © ADRIAN DENNIS/AFP/Getty Images; **page 6** © andyross/iStock/Thinkstock; **page 12** © Daniel Swee/Alamy Stock Photo; **page 15** © photosbyjim/iStock/Thinkstock; **page 24** © warrengoldswain/iStock/Thinkstock; **page 25** © RIA Novosti/TopFoto; **page 29** © Wavebreak Media/ Thinkstock; **page 33** © DigitalVision/Thinkstock; **page 35** © LUNAMARINA/iStock/Thinkstock; **page 36** (top) © FR Sport Photography/Alamy Stock Photo, (bottom) © Crdjan/iStock/Thinkstock; **page 38** © BSIP/UIG Via Getty Images; **pages 41 & 43** © David Noton Photography/Alamy Stock Photo; **page 47** © Leo Mason sports photos/Alamy Stock Photo; **page 48** © Demid/iStock/Thinkstock; **page 50** © Morne de Klerk/Getty Images; **page 51** © ShariffC/iStock/ Thinkstock; **page 52** © BanksPhotos/E+/Getty Images; **page 53** © Sergejs Nescereckis/Alamy Stock Photo; **page 55** © Gero Breloer/dpa picture alliance archive/Alamy Stock Photo; **page 56** © PIKSEL/iStock/Thinkstock; **page 58** © Mark Dadswell/Getty Images; **page 62** © Songbird839/iStock/Thinkstock; **page 68** © lightpoet/123RF; **page 71** © Michael Dodge/Getty Images; **page 72** © Wavebreak Media Ltd/123RF; **page 73** © Craig Brown/Photographer's Choice RF/ Getty Images; **page 74** © ALAN EDWARDS/Alamy Stock Photo; **page 77** © Andrew Lloyd/Alamy Stock Photo; **page 80** © PHILIPPE DESMAZES/AFP/Getty Images; **pages 85 & 94** © Gero Breloer/dpa picture alliance archive/Alamy Stock Photo; **page 91** © Dennis MacDonald/Alamy Stock Photo; **page 92** © txking/iStock/Thinkstock; **page 98** © Juergen Hasenkopf/Alamy Stock Photo; **page 99** © moodboard/Thinkstock; **page 100** © GeoPic/Alamy Stock Photo; **page 108** © Fred van Wijk/Alamy Stock Photo; **page 112** © Steve Bardens/The RFU Collection/Getty Images; **page 114** © ARMANDO BABANI/epa european pressphoto agency b.v./Alamy Stock Photo; **page 118** © Sport Picture Library/ Alamy Stock Photo; **pages 121 & 128** © Robbie Stephenson/Telephoto Images/Alamy Stock Photo; **page 123** (left) © Cem Oksuz/Anadolu Agency/Getty Images, (right) © Aflo/REX/Shutterstock; **page 125** © Visage/Stockbyte/Getty Images; **page 129** (top) © Ron Chapple Studios/Thinkstock, (bottom) © Action Plus Sports Images/Alamy Stock Photo; **page 131** © Mike Booth/Alamy Stock Photo; **page 133** © Sport In Pictures/Alamy Stock Photo; **page 135** © Robert Cianflone/Getty Images; **page 137** © Chad Case/Alamy Stock Photo; **page 139** © Fuse/Thinkstock; **pages 143 & 157** © Antonio_Diaz/iStock/Thinkstock; **page 145** © monkeybusinessimages/iStock/Thinkstock; **page 146** © Ljupco/iStock/ Thinkstock; **page 151** © minadezhda/iStock/Thinkstock

Every effort has been made to trace all copyright holders, but if any have been inadvertently overlooked, the Publishers will be pleased to make the necessary arrangements at the first opportunity.

Although every effort has been made to ensure that website addresses are correct at time of going to press, Hodder Education cannot be held responsible for the content of any website mentioned in this book. It is sometimes possible to find a relocated web page by typing in the address of the home page for a website in the URL window of your browser.

Hachette UK's policy is to use papers that are natural, renewable and recyclable products and made from wood grown in sustainable forests. The logging and manufacturing processes are expected to conform to the environmental regulations of the country of origin.

Orders: please contact Bookpoint Ltd, 130 Park Drive, Milton Park, Abingdon, Oxon OX14 4SE. Telephone: +44 (0)1235 827720. Fax: +44 (0)1235 400454. Email education@bookpoint.co.uk Lines are open from 9 a.m. to 5 p.m., Monday to Saturday, with a 24-hour message answering service. You can also order through our website: www.hoddereducation.co.uk

ISBN: 978 1 4718 5172 8

© John Honeybourne 2016

First published in 2009

This second edition published in 2016 by

Hodder Education,

An Hachette UK Company

Carmelite House

50 Victoria Embankment

London EC4Y 0DZ

www.hoddereducation.co.uk

Impression number   10 9 8 7 6

Year   2020 2019

Cover photo © Michael Krinke/istockphoto.com

Typeset in Myriad Pro 12/14pt by Aptara Inc.

Printed in Italy

A catalogue record for this title is available from the British Library.

Contents

Introduction

This OCR endorsed textbook is designed specifically to cover the specification content for the OCR GCSE Physical Education qualification (J587). Each part in the book covers a different main topic area of the OCR specification and each chapter explores in more detail the specification content, along with material that will fully develop each candidate's understanding of each topic area. The book includes extension material to stretch and challenge candidates and to give context to the theoretical principles covered.

How to use this book

Understanding the Specification

Outline of the main ways the content is related to the specification.

IN THE NEWS

References to contemporary real-life events and are designed to demonstrate the important of PE to the world around us.

Key terms

A short definition of key vocabulary

❓ Extend your knowledge

Extension material for each chapter that might go slightly beyond the specification but give extra information for possible use in extended answers.

Activities

Short tasks and activities to help reinforce learning.

✔ Check your understanding

Short, knowledge-based questions to help you check you've understood different topics.

Practice questions

Questions designed to offer study practice.

STUDY HINTS

Handy tips for studying PE.

SUMMARY

Summary of key points of each chapter.

Section 1
Applied Anatomy and Physiology

Chapter 1.1
The structure and function of the skeletal system

Understanding the Specification

This topic area will help you know and understand the location of the major bones in the body. By the end of the topic you will be able to apply examples to the functions of the skeleton. You should know the major joints and the articulating bones (bones that make up the joint) in the knee, elbow, shoulder and hip. You should also know about types of movements at hinge joints and ball and socket joints and be able to use practical examples to show and analyse different movements.

Activity

Write the names of the major bones of the body on separate Post-it Notes. With a partner, put each Post-it on the appropriate area for the bone.

Location of the major bones

More than 200 bones make up the human skeleton. For us to understand how the body moves effectively in sports activities, it is important to know the location of the main bones.

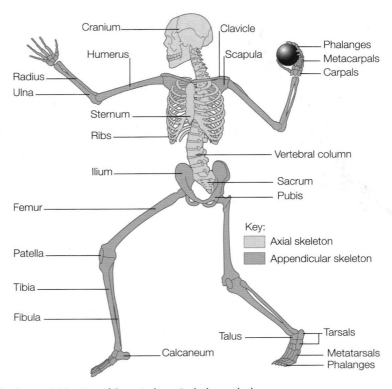

❓ Extend your knowledge

The **axial skeleton** is the central part of the skeleton and is the main source of support. It includes the cranium (the skull), the vertebral column (bones that make up the spine) and the rib cage, including 12 pairs of ribs and the sternum.
The **appendicular skeleton** consists of the remaining bones and includes the structures that join these bones on to the axial skeleton.

▲ Figure 1.1.1 Location of the major bones in the human body

You should know the location of the following bones:

- cranium
- vertebrae
- ribs
- sternum
- clavicle
- scapula
- humerus
- ulna
- radius
- carpals
- metacarpals
- phalanges
- pelvis (ilium)
- femur
- patella
- tibia
- fibula
- tarsals
- metatarsals.

Functions of the skeleton

The skeleton has several major functions:

1. To give shape and support to the body – therefore giving the body posture.
2. To allow movement of the body – by providing areas or sites for muscle attachment. This also provides for a system of levers that helps us move.
3. To give protection to the internal organs – such as heart, lungs, spinal cord and the brain. For example, the cranium protects the brain.
4. To produce blood – red and white blood cells.
5. To store minerals – such as phosphorus, calcium, potassium and iron, etc. Iron helps in the transport of oxygen to working muscles and calcium is needed to build and repair bones.

Types of synovial joint

A joint is where two or more bones meet. There are many different types of joint in the human body, including some that do not allow movement, or allow very little. Joints are very important in movements related to sport. The type of joint that we are more concerned with is the **synovial joint**. This is the most common joint and since it allows for a wide range of movement is very important to people playing sports. It consists of a joint capsule, lined with a synovial membrane. There is lubrication provided for the joint in the form of synovial fluid. This is secreted into the joint, e.g. the knee joint, by the synovial membrane.

Key term

Synovial joint This is a freely movable joint in which the bones' surfaces are covered by cartilage, called articular cartilage, and connected by a fibrous connective tissue capsule (joint capsule) lined with synovial fluid.

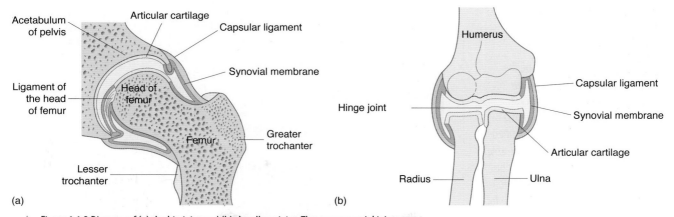

Acetabulum of pelvis
Articular cartilage
Capsular ligament
Synovial membrane
Ligament of the head of femur
Head of femur
Femur
Greater trochanter
Lesser trochanter
(a)

Humerus
Capsular ligament
Synovial membrane
Hinge joint
Articular cartilage
Radius
Ulna
(b)

▲ Figure 1.1.2 Diagram of (a) the hip joint and (b) the elbow joint. These are synovial joints

The many different categories for joints relate to the degree of movement that they allow, ranging from fibrous (fixed) to synovial (allowing significant movement). Synovial joints are then further categorised into the type of movement they allow, whether rotational, hinged (hinge) or from side to side (on a plane).

❓ Extend your knowledge

Other types of joint are:

- **Fibrous or fixed**: this does not allow any movement. There is tough, fibrous tissue that lays between the ends of the bones, e.g. the sutures or thin joints of the cranium.

- **Cartilaginous or slightly movable**: this allows some movement. The ends of the bones have tough fibrous cartilage, which allows for shock absorption but also gives stability, e.g. the joints in the spine called intervertebral discs.

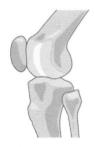

▲ Figure 1.1.3 The knee joint is used extensively in sport and exercise

Key term

Articulating bones These are the bones that move within a joint.

Hinge joint

The hinge joint allows movement in one plane only, just like a door hinge moves (uniaxial), e.g. knee joint and elbow joint. An example of a physical activity that uses the knee joint is sprinting. For the elbow joint a physical activity is the biceps curl in weight training.

The **articulating bones** for the elbow joint are the:

- humerus
- radius
- ulna.

Ball and socket joint

This allows a wide range of movement and occurs when a round head of bone fits into a cup-shaped depression, e.g. the shoulder joint and the hip joint. An example of a physical activity that uses the shoulder joint is an athlete throwing a javelin. An example of a physical activity that uses the hip joint is a sit-up training exercise.

STUDY HINT

Make sure that you can describe the hinge joint (using knee and elbow examples) and the ball and socket joint (using shoulder and hip joints) in particular because these are identified in the specification. You need to be able to give examples of each and describe movements that are associated with the use of each of these two joints – for example, the biceps curl for the elbow, the squat movement for the knee, the bowling action for the shoulder and the sit-up action for the hip.

▲ Figure 1.1.4 The thrower needs a healthy and strong shoulder joint

The articulating bones for the shoulder joint are the:
- humerus
- scapula.

The articulating bones for the hip joint are the:
- pelvis
- femur.

Types of movement at hinge joints and ball and socket joints

There are different types of movement associated with the joints in our bodies, including:
- flexion
- extension
- rotation
- abduction
- adduction.

Movement at hinge joints

Flexion is a decrease in the angle around a joint.

- **At the knee**: for example, bending your leg at the knee when preparing to make a pass in football.
- **At the elbow**: bending your arm at the elbow and touching your shoulder with your hand – for example, when a badminton player prepares to hit an overhead clear, the arm shows flexion at the elbow.

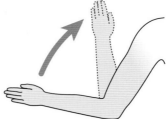

▲ Figure 1.1.5 Flexion at the elbow

Extension is when the angle of the bones that are moving (articulating bones) is increased.

- **At the knee**: from a stooped or squat position you then stand up. The angle between your femur and tibia (upper and lower leg) increases, thus extension has taken place – for example, when a basketball player drives up to the basket from bent legs to straight, extension occurs at the knee joint.
- **At the elbow**: straightening your arm at the elbow joint. The angle between the humerus and the radius/ulna (upper and lower arm) is increased, thus extension takes place – for example, when making a basketball set shot the bent arm moves to a straight arm as you release the ball and extension occurs at the elbow joint.

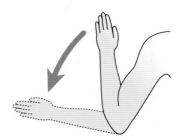

▲ Figure 1.1.6 Extension at the elbow

▲ Figure 1.1.7 A ballet dancer moves into first position and rotates the hip joint laterally

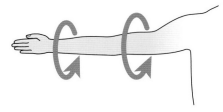

▲ Figure 1.1.8 Rotation at the shoulder

Movement at ball and socket joints

Flexion:

- **At the shoulder**: involves movement of the arm forwards and up overhead – for example, lifting the arms out of the water during the backstroke in swimming.
- **At the hip**: describes the bending motion that brings your thigh toward your chest – for example, in hockey, bending down to ensure that your hockey stick is flat on the floor and can stop the ball.

Extension:

- **At the shoulder**: is the lowering of the arm from in front and taking it back behind you – for example, the execution of a serve in tennis, when the player takes the arm back before throwing the ball up.
- **At the hip**: moving the leg backwards towards the posterior side of the body – for example, a rugby player extends the hip in preparation for kicking through the ball, to get maximum power.

Rotation is when the bone turns about its longitudinal axis within the joint. Rotation towards the body is called internal or medial rotation; rotation away from the body is called external or lateral rotation. For example:

- **Hip**: a ballet dancer moves into first position and rotates the hip joint laterally.
- **Shoulder**: a tennis player uses external rotation at the shoulder joint during the backswing of the serve.

Abduction is the movement of the body away from the middle or the midline of the body – for example:

- **Hip**: a gymnast with her leg lifted to the side of her body shows abduction.
- **Shoulder**: a swimmer lifts the arms out to the side during the butterfly stroke.

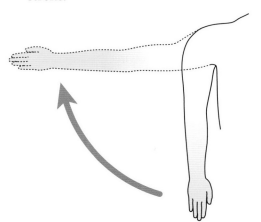

▲ Figure 1.1.9 Abduction at the shoulder

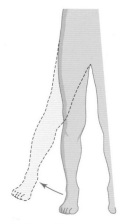

▲ Figure 1.1.10 Abduction of the leg at the hip

Adduction is the opposite of abduction and is the movement towards the midline of the body, e.g. lowering your lifted leg that you have abducted towards the middle of your body – for example:

- **Hip**: in swimming the recovery of the legs from the breaststroke leg kick involves adduction.

- **Shoulder**: a rugby player tackling another player will hold on to the player by adducting her arms as she tackles.

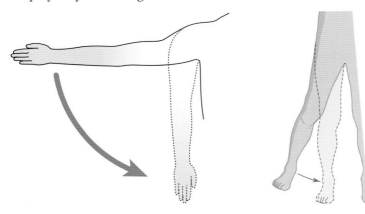

▲ Figure 1.1.11 Adduction at the shoulder   ▲ Figure 1.1.12 Adduction at the hip

Circumduction is a combination of abduction, adduction, extension or flexion and rotation. It describes a continuous circular movement of a limb around a joint:

- **Hip**: a gymnast on the beam takes her back leg off the beam and moves it out and round to place her foot ahead of her front foot.
- **Shoulder**: a swimmer during the front crawl arm action will take their arm out and round and back into the water, showing circumduction at the shoulder joint.

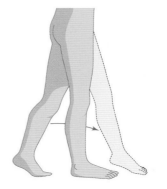

▲ Figure 1.1.13 Circumduction at the hip

Activity

Sketch a simple diagram of the knee joint and label the bones that move around this joint.

Name a physical activity that involves both flexion and extension of the knee joint.

Draw the hip joint and label the bones that move around this joint.

Describe a skill in a physical activity that involves both abduction and adduction of the hip joint.

Other components of joints

There are three other main components of joints that it is helpful for budding athletes to know about. These are:

- ligaments
- cartilage
- tendons.

In the same way that joints link the various bones in our body, these tissue-based components help to reduce wear and tear in a variety of ways, for example by absorbing shock or reducing friction.

Ligaments

These are found between bones and attach bone to bone. They are bands of connective tissue that are very tough and resilient.

- **Function**: the role of ligaments is to help join bones together and keep the joints stable during movement.

Some ligaments lie within the synovial capsule, others are outside the capsule. The ligaments prevent movements that are extreme and help stop dislocation.

Cartilage

This is soft connective tissue.

- **Function**: the role of cartilage is to reduce friction and act as a shock absorber for the joint.

Newly born babies have a skeleton consisting of cartilage and as they get older this cartilage is mostly replaced by bone, a process known as ossification. Bones have a blood supply, but cartilage has no blood supply. There are three basic types of cartilage:

- **Yellow elastic cartilage**: flexible tissue, e.g. part of the ear lobe.
- **Hyaline or blue articular cartilage**: found on the articulating surfaces of bones, it protects and allows movement between bones with limited friction and therefore more flexibility. Hyaline cartilage can thicken as a result of exercise.
- **White fibro-cartilage**: consists of tough tissue that acts as a shock absorber. It is found in parts of the body where there is a great amount of stress, for example the semi-lunar cartilage in the knee joint. It also allows bones to fit together properly; for example, as discs between the vertebrae.

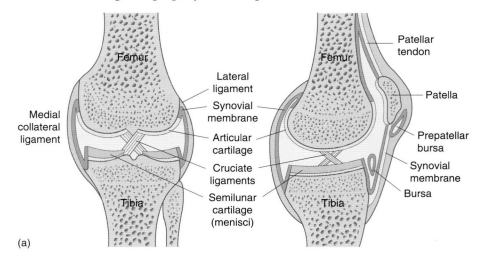

(a)

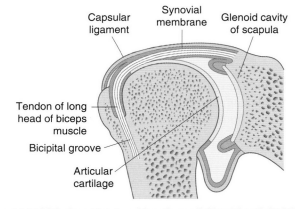

(b)

▲ Figure 1.1.14 (a) The knee joint viewed from the rear (left) and the side (right) and (b) the shoulder joint

You may tear a cartilage with a forceful knee movement. For example, a footballer may twist the knee while their foot is still on the ground, perhaps while dribbling round a defender. Or a tennis player may twist to hit a ball hard but keep their foot in the same position.

Sometimes a tear develops due to repeated small injuries to the cartilage, or to degeneration ('wear and tear') of the **meniscus cartilage** in older people. In severe injuries, other parts of the knee may be damaged in addition to a meniscus tear – for example, you may also sprain or tear a ligament.

The cartilage does not heal very well once it is torn. This is mainly because it does not have a good blood supply. So, some small outer tears may heal in time, but larger tears, or a tear in the middle of the knee cartilage, tend not to heal properly.

Tendons

Muscles are attached to bones via tendons. These are strong and can be a little flexible.

- **Function**: As well as their attachment role, they help to transmit the power needed to move bones. When a muscle shortens, it pulls on the tendons; this pulls on the bones to which the tendons are attached and causes movement.

Key term

Meniscus cartilage In the knee, these are areas of cartilage tissue that act like shock absorbers in the joint.

IN THE NEWS

Achilles tendons play a critical role in human running ability, the Festival of Science in York has been told. A new computer model confirms that skeletons need to store energy in their tendons to be able to run efficiently.

❓ Extend your knowledge

If contraction is excessively strong then tendons can be damaged. For example, the Achilles tendon is found in the lower leg and can be damaged. If the tendon is damaged below the knee, often caused by over training, then **Osgood-Schlatter's disease** could be experienced.

Key term

Osgood-Schlatter's disease This is a common cause of knee pain in children and is linked to bone and muscle growth.

An active, healthy lifestyle that is balanced in the amount and type of exercise undertaken can limit the damage that may be caused to tendons. Exercise can strengthen tendons and make them less prone to injury.

SUMMARY

- The main functions of the skeleton are to give shape and support to the body, to allow movement of the body, to give protection to the internal organs, to produce blood cells and to store minerals.
- A synovial joint is a freely movable joint in which the bony surfaces are covered by articular cartilage and connected by a fibrous connective tissue capsule lined with a synovial membrane.
- The articulating bones for the knee joint are the femur and the tibia. The articulating bones for the elbow joint are the humerus, the radius and the ulna. The articulating bones for the shoulder joint are the humerus and the scapula.
- Flexion is a decrease in the angle around a joint. Extension is when the angle of the bones that are moving (articulating bones) is increased. Rotation is when the bone turns about its longitudinal axis within the joint.
- Abduction is the movement of the body away from the middle or the midline of the body. Adduction is the opposite of abduction and is the movement towards the midline of the body.
- Circumduction is a combination of abduction, adduction, extension or flexion and rotation. It describes a continuous circular movement of a limb around a joint.
- The role of ligaments is to help join bones together and keep the joints stable during movement. The role of cartilage is to reduce friction and act as a shock absorber for the joint.
- Muscles are attached to bones via tendons. As well as their attachment role, they help to transmit the power needed to move bones.

Practice questions

1. Describe the main functions of the skeleton.   **(5 marks)**
2. Give two examples of a hinge joint and two examples of a ball and socket joint.   **(4 marks)**
3. What is the difference between adduction and abduction? Give an example for each.   **(4 marks)**
4. Describe the role of tendons.   **(3 marks)**

Chapter 1.2
The structure and function of the muscular system

Understanding the Specification

This topic area will teach you the name and location of the main muscle groups in the human body and you will be able to apply them to examples from physical activity/ sport. You will know the definitions and roles of the:

- agonist
- antagonist
- fixator
- antagonistic muscle action.

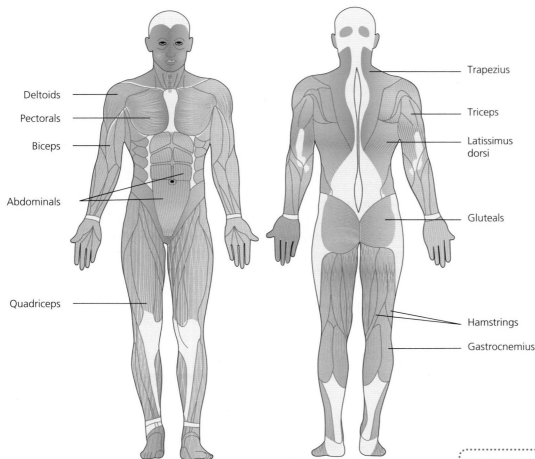

Deltoids
Pectorals
Biceps
Abdominals
Quadriceps

Trapezius
Triceps
Latissimus dorsi
Gluteals
Hamstrings
Gastrocnemius

▲ Figure 1.2.1 The main muscle groups in the human body

Muscles are made up of soft muscle tissue and skeletal muscle enables us to move. In sport the study of muscle and how it works gives us a good insight into how we might make our sports skills and activities even more effective and efficient.

STUDY HINT
Be able to locate each of these major muscle groups and label an appropriate diagram showing the position of each muscle group. Also know the main role of each of these groups by using an example from sport.

The location of major muscle groups

The following muscles are named in the specification:

- **Deltoid** – this is used in all movements of the arms. Its most important function is to lift the arm straight outwards and upwards (abduction at shoulder joint), e.g. to make a block in volleyball with arms straight above the head.
- **Trapezius** – this causes extension at the neck, e.g a rugby forward in a scrum will use the trapezius to bind into the opponents.
- **Latissimus dorsi** – this is the broad back muscle. It causes adduction at the shoulder joint. It will swing the arm backwards and rotate it inwards. For example, a tennis player who swings their arm back to hit the ball when serving is using the latissimus dorsi.
- **Pectorals** – there are two sets of chest muscles: pectoralis major (greater chest muscle) and pectoralis minor (lesser chest muscle). This causes adduction and flexion at the shoulder joint in the horizontal plane. These help to adduct the arm and rotate it inwards as well as lowering the shoulder blades, e.g. a rugby player making a tackle would hold on to their opponent using the pectoral muscles.
- **Biceps** (biceps brachii) – this causes flexion at the elbow. Its function is to swing the upper arm forward and to turn the forearm so that the palm of the hand points upwards (supination), e.g. biceps curl in weight training.
- **Triceps** (triceps brachii) – this causes extension at the elbow. Its function is to straighten the elbow and to swing the arm backwards, e.g. backhand in table tennis.
- **Abdominals** – these bend the body forwards at the hips causing flexion of vertebral column and help to turn the upper body. For example, performing a sit-up exercise will use the abdominals.
- **Quadriceps** – this provides stability to the knee joint and extends or straightens the knee joint. For example, a long jumper when driving off the board will straighten the knee joint at take-off using the quadriceps.
- **Hamstrings** – these muscles will straighten the hip and cause flexion at the knee joint. They will also bend the knee and rotate it outwards. For example, a hockey player running across the pitch will be using her hamstrings in the running action to bend the knees.

▲ Figure 1.2.2 A hockey player will use her hamstrings to bend the knees when she runs

Activity

Write the names of the major muscle groups on Post-its and with a partner place each Post-it on each other's body showing that you know the location. Or use a diagram and identify the major muscle groups. This could be made into giant posters for the classroom walls and help you to remember the locations of these muscle groups.

❓ Extend your knowledge

There are three types of muscle:

- Involuntary muscle – or smooth muscle, which is found in the body's internal organs. This is involuntary muscle because it is not under our conscious control.
- Cardiac muscle – this is found in the heart only and is also involuntary.
- Skeletal or voluntary muscle – this is under our conscious control and is used primarily for movement, e.g. the biceps muscle in our arms.

- **Gluteals** – these are the muscles in your buttocks. They cause extension at the hip joint and adduct the hip, rotate the thigh outwards and helps to straighten the knee. A sprinter will use the gluteals in the leg action of sprinting down the track.
- **Gastrocnemius** – the calf muscle is used to bend the knee and to straighten or plantarflex the ankle. For example, a swimmer doing front crawl will point their toes in the leg action using the gastrocnemius.

The roles of muscles in movement

Pairs of muscles

There is a vast range of movements that can be made by the human body. To produce these movements, muscles either shorten, lengthen or remain the same length when they contract. Muscles work in pairs: as one muscle contracts, the other relaxes. Muscles that work together like this are called **antagonistic pairs**. This type of action enables the body to move with stability and control.

Examples of antagonistic pairs are:

- **Biceps and triceps** – at the elbow joint. As the biceps bends or flexes the elbow joint by contracting, the triceps relaxes. As the arm straightens, the opposite occurs.
- **Hamstrings and quadriceps** – at the knee joint. The hamstrings contract and the quadriceps relax and the knee joint flexes. As the knee joint extends, the quadriceps (quads) contract and the hamstrings relax.

Agonist

This is the working muscle that produces or controls the desired joint movement. It is also known as the **prime mover**. For example, the biceps brachii is the muscle that produces the flexion movement at the elbow.

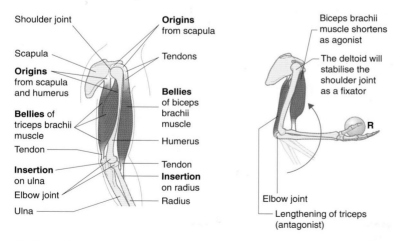

▲ Figure 1.2.3 Flexion at the elbow with agonist labelled

Key terms

Origin This is the end of the muscle attached to a bone that is stable, e.g. the scapula. The point of origin remains still when contraction occurs.

Insertion This is the end of the muscle attached to the bone that actively moves, e.g. the biceps insertion is on the radius.

Antagonist

For movement to be co-ordinated, muscles work in pairs so that control is maintained. The movement caused by the agonist is countered by the action of the opposing muscle, called the antagonist. For example, the flexion at the elbow caused by the biceps shortening is opposed by the lengthening of the triceps, which acts as the antagonist, which is the relaxing muscle.

Fixator

This is a muscle that works with others to stabilise the origin of the prime mover, e.g. the trapezius contracts to stabilise the **origin** of the biceps. Some muscles have two or more origins, e.g. the biceps muscle has two heads that pull on the one **insertion** to lift the lower arm.

❓ Extend your knowledge

Synergists

These refer to muscles that are actively helping the prime mover or agonist to produce the desired movement. They are sometimes called **neutralisers** because they prevent any undesired movements. Sometimes the fixator and the synergist are the same muscle, e.g. the brachialis acts as a synergist when the elbow is bent and the forearm moves upwards.

SUMMARY

- The agonist, also known as the prime mover, is the working muscle and produces the desired joint movement, e.g. the biceps brachii produces flexion at the elbow.
- The role of the antagonist is to counter or oppose the action of the agonist.
- The fixator works with others to stabilise the joint.
- Antagonistic muscle action is when muscles work in pairs. As one muscle contracts, the other relaxes.

Practice questions

1. Label a diagram showing the major muscle groups.
   (11 marks)
2. Using an example from sport, describe how the biceps and triceps work as an antagonistic pair. **(4 marks)**
3. What is meant by a fixator? **(2 marks)**
4. What are the main functions of the following muscle groups? **(4 marks)**
   - Quadriceps
   - Gastrocnemius
   - Abdominals
   - Pectorals.

Chapter 1.3
Movement analysis

Lever systems

Levers are important in movement because they allow efficiency and force to be applied to the body's movements.

Many bones and muscles act together to form levers. A lever is a rigid structure, a length of bone that turns about a pivot – the joint.

Levers are used to make a small amount of force into a much bigger force. This is known as gaining **mechanical advantage**.

There are four parts to a lever: lever arm, pivot, effort and load.

- Bones act as lever arms.
- Joints act as pivots.
- Muscles provide the effort to move loads.
- Load forces are often the weight of the body parts that are moved or forces needed to lift, push or pull things.

Levers can also be used to increase the force of movement. For example, when throwing a javelin, small contractions of arm and back muscles produce a much greater force of movement at the end of the arm.

Key term

Mechanical advantage Some levers (first class and second class) provide mechanical advantage. This means that they allow you to move a large output load with a smaller effort. Load and effort are forces and are measured in Newtons (N). Mechanical advantage is calculated as follows:

Mechanical advantage = Load ÷ Effort

For example, where the load = 500 N and the effort = 100 N, the mechanical advantage would be:

$$500 \text{ N} ÷ 100 \text{ N} = 5$$

▲ Figure 1.3.1 Levers can be used to increase the force of movement

IN THE NEWS

Sports scientists are continuing to help fly halves in rugby to modify and improve their kicking technique. The use of biomechanics (how the body moves), such as how levers work and the planes of movement, has been key in helping players understand the principles behind their sports activities.

> **STUDY HINT**
> Make sure you can define each class of lever and that you can use the following joints in appropriate practical examples: neck; ankle; elbow.

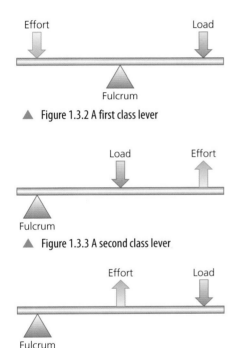

▲ Figure 1.3.2 A first class lever

▲ Figure 1.3.3 A second class lever

▲ Figure 1.3.4 A third class lever

There are three classes or types of lever. Some levers operate differently to others.

1. **First class levers** – the fulcrum (sometimes called the pivot) is located between the effort force and the load force on the lever arm. First class levers can increase both the effects of the effort and the speed of a body. An example of this type of lever is the neck joint.
    *   **Practical example**: At the neck – heading a ball in football. A see-saw in a playground is another example of a first class lever where the effort balances the load.

2. **Second class levers** – this is when the load or resistance is between the fulcrum and the effort. Second class levers tend only to increase the effect of the effort force. If you raise up on your toes or plantar flex at the ankle, the second class lever comes into operation.
    *   **Practical example**: At the ankle – standing on tip toes when reaching for a smash in badminton.

3. **Third class levers** – this is when the effort is between the fulcrum and the load or resistance. Third class levers can be used to increase the speed of a body. This is the most common form of lever in the human body.
    *   **Practical example**: At the elbow – the action of the biceps and the triceps at the elbow joint when performing a biceps curl.
    *   At the knee – the action of the hamstrings and the quadriceps at the knee joint causing flexion and extension, such as leaping up to catch a basketball.

Planes of movement

To be able to explain how the body moves, it is useful to see the body as having imaginary lines or planes running through it. These planes divide the body in three ways:

*   Frontal plane
*   Transverse plane
*   Sagittal plane.

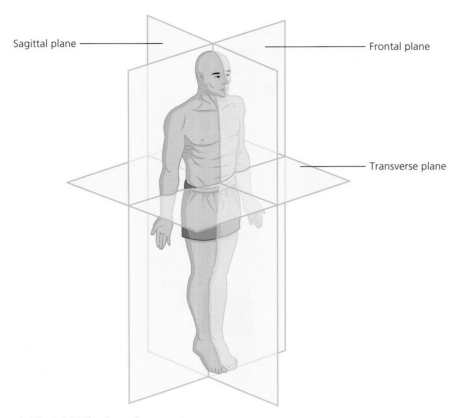

▲ Figure 1.3.5 The planes of movement

Frontal plane

The frontal plane runs vertically and divides the body in sections, between front (anterior) and back (posterior). Movements in this plane are sideways movements of abduction and adduction.

- **Application to a practical example**: abduction and adduction of the legs at the hip joint, e.g. performing 'jumping jack' type exercises, or action at the hip during the breast stroke leg action in swimming.

Transverse plane

The transverse plane divides the body into upper or superior section and lower or inferior section. Movements in this plane are rotational.

- **Application to a practical example**: arm action (circumduction) when bowling in cricket with rotation at the shoulder joint.

Sagittal plane

The sagittal plane splits the body vertically into left and right sides. Movements in this plane are the up and down movements of flexion and extension.

- **Application to a practical example**: leg action in running takes place in a sagittal plane.

> **? Extend your knowledge**
>
> Multi-planar movement is the body working in all planes and can be a good full-body workout. A dancer can spin, leap and bend in a multi-planar activity. Many movements in sports activities involve movements that are multi-planar.

Axes of rotation

An axis is a straight line around which an object rotates. The movement at a joint takes place in a plane about an axis.

There are three **axes of rotation**:

- frontal axis
- transverse axis
- longitudinal axis.

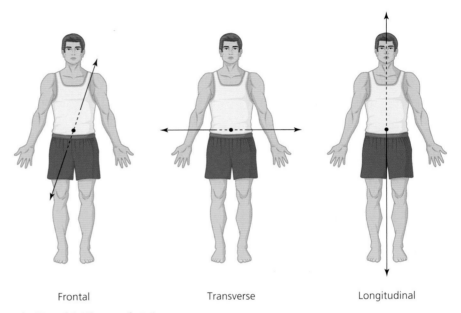

Frontal   Transverse   Longitudinal

▲ Figure 1.3.6 The axes of rotation

▼ Table 1.3.1a Movements with their dominant planes

Plane	Movement
Frontal	Adduction/ Abduction
Transverse	Rotation
Saggital	Flexion/ Extension

▼ Table 1.3.1b Activity examples with their axes of rotation

Axis	Example
Transverse (side to side)	Somersault
Longitudinal (top to bottom)	Pirouette in Dance
Frontal (Back to Front)	Cartwheel

STUDY HINT

Link a plane of movement to an axis of rotation for a variety of activities other than those shown in the example above. Examination questions are likely to ask for locations of each axis and for a practical example for each. Use diagrams for each axis to help you to remember.

SUMMARY

- Levers are important in movement because they allow efficiency and force to be applied to the body's movements.
- First class and second class levers can both provide mechanical advantage.
- First class levers – the fulcrum is located between the effort force and the load force.
- Second class levers – this is when the load or resistance is between the fulcrum and the effort.
- Third class levers – this is when the effort is between the fulcrum and the load or resistance.
- The frontal plane runs vertically and divides the body in sections, between front (anterior) and back (posterior). Movements in the frontal plane are abduction and adduction.
- The transverse plane divides the body into upper or superior section and lower or inferior section. Movements in the transverse plane are rotational.
- The sagittal plane splits the body vertically into left and right sides. Movements in the sagittal plane are the up and down movements of flexion and extension.
- An axis is a straight line around which an object rotates. There are three axes of rotation:
  - frontal (front to back) axis
  - transverse (side to side) axis
  - longitudinal (top to bottom) axis.

Practice questions

1. Give the three classes of lever. **(3 marks)**
2. Explain what is meant by mechanical advantage. **(2 marks)**
3. Draw a simple diagram showing the three planes of movement. **(3 marks)**
4. Using three different practical examples, describe the axes of rotation. **(6 marks)**

Chapter 1.4
The cardiovascular and respiratory systems

Understanding the Specification

In this large topic area you will learn about the structure and function of the cardiovascular system, including the double circulatory system (systemic and pulmonary). You will know the different types of blood vessels and understand the pathway of blood through the heart. You will know the definitions of heart rate, stroke volume and cardiac output as well as learning about the role of red blood cells. This topic area also covers the structure and function of the respiratory system and you will understand the pathway of air through the respiratory system as well as knowing the role of respiratory muscles in breathing. You will need to understand the definitions of breathing rate, tidal volume and minute ventilation and understand about alveoli as the site of gaseous exchange. This topic area includes the definitions of aerobic and anaerobic exercise and you should be able to apply practical examples of aerobic and anaerobic activities in relation to intensity and duration.

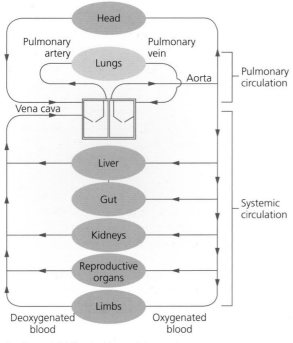

▲ Figure 1.4.1 The double circulatory system

Structure and function of the cardiovascular system

Both the heart and the blood vessels are crucial for anyone who wishes to improve their fitness for sport. A good working knowledge of these will enable an athlete to identify how the body can be helped to work harder and for longer.

The double circulatory system

Blood in the body continuously flows through a network of blood vessels that forms a double circuit. This circuit connects the heart to the lungs and then the heart to the other organs in the body. This double circuit involves pulmonary circulation and systemic circulation.

The pulmonary system

This involves the transportation of blood between the lungs and the heart. The pulmonary artery takes deoxygenated blood from the right ventricle of the heart to the lungs. In the lungs the blood becomes oxygenated and off-loads carbon dioxide. The pulmonary vein then takes the oxygenated blood back to the left atrium of the heart.

The systemic system

The blood is pumped from the left ventricle of the heart into the aorta. The blood is then transported to the rest of the body via arteries. Veins return the blood, which is low in oxygen and high in carbon dioxide, to the heart. The blood then enters the right atrium via the vena cava.

STUDY HINT

Be able to draw a simple diagram of the double circulatory system and be able to describe the pulmonary and systemic elements of this double system. See Figure 1.4.2 for an example.

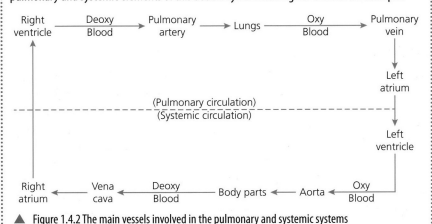

▲ Figure 1.4.2 The main vessels involved in the pulmonary and systemic systems

Blood and blood vessels

Blood vessels are an integral part of the **cardiovascular** system and are essential for the transportation of material around the body. During exercise, most of the blood goes to the working muscles so that oxygen can be delivered and carbon dioxide taken away efficiently and effectively, which is important when the body is exercising.

Blood consists of cells and is surrounded by a liquid called plasma. The total blood volume in the average male is five to six litres and the blood volume in the average female is four to five litres. Blood also consists of erythrocytes, which are red corpuscles (cells) containing **haemoglobin**. Blood also consists of leucocytes, which are white blood cells that combat infection, and thrombocytes (platelets), which are important in the process of blood clotting.

The vascular system includes blood vessels called:

- arteries
- arterioles
- capillaries
- veins
- venules.

The specification covers the three main vessels of arteries, capillaries and veins.

The role of red blood cells

Red blood cells, or erythrocytes, are the most abundant blood cells. The primary function of red blood cells is to transport oxygen to cells around the body and to deliver carbon dioxide to the lungs.

Arteries

These are blood vessels that carry blood at high pressure from the heart to the body tissues. The largest artery is called the aorta, which leaves the heart and subdivides into smaller vessels. The smaller of these are

Key terms

Cardiovascular Cardio means heart, vascular means circulatory networks of the blood vessels.

Haemoglobin This is iron-rich protein found in red blood cells and transports oxygen in the blood. The more concentrated the haemoglobin, the more oxygen can be carried. This concentration can be increased through endurance training.

❓ Extend your knowledge

A red blood cell has what is known as a biconcave shape. Both sides of the cell's surface curve inwards like the interior of a sphere. This shape aids in a red blood cell's ability to deliver oxygen to body tissues.

Red blood cells are also important in establishing blood type. Blood type is determined by the presence or absence of **antigens** on the surface of red blood cells.

Key term

Antigen Substance that causes your immune system to produce antibodies that fight disease.

Key terms

Vasodilation This occurs when the artery walls increase their diameter.

Vasoconstriction This occurs when the artery walls decrease their diameter.

called arterioles and have a very small diameter. The walls of arteries contain smooth muscle tissue, which enables the vessels to increase (**vasodilation**) or decrease their diameter (**vasoconstriction**). This then controls the blood flow and therefore the amount of oxygen that is delivered to body tissues.

By increasing and decreasing their diameter, the vessels in arteries can therefore help to change the pressure of the blood, which is especially important during exercise.

Veins

These carry blood at low pressure and return the blood to the heart. Their walls are less muscular but gradually increase in thickness as they approach the heart. The vena cava is the largest vein, which enters the heart through the right atrium. The smallest veins are called venules and these transport the blood from the capillaries. Veins contain pocket valves that prevent the backflow of blood.

Capillaries

These have only a single layer of cells in their walls. This makes them thin enough for nutrients and waste products to pass through them. Capillaries occur in large quantities around the muscles and this enables effective exchange of gases.

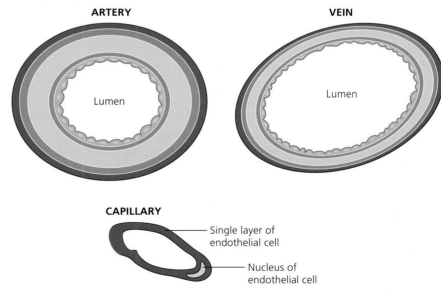

▲ Figure 1.4.3 The three main types of blood vessels – arteries, veins, and capillaries

Extend your knowledge

The muscular wall of the heart is called the myocardium and is found between the inner endocardium and the outer membrane called the pericardium.

The two chambers at the superior (top) part of the heart are called **atria**. The two inferior (lower) chambers are called **ventricles**.

The heart and the pathway of blood

The heart is part of the cardiovascular system. About the size of a closed fist, it consists of four chambers and is made up almost entirely of cardiac muscle. The heart can be seen as incorporating two separate pumps, whose main function is to pump blood around the body. The right-side pump sends deoxygenated blood to the lungs, while the left-side pump sends oxygenated blood to the body's muscles. A muscular wall called a septum separates these two pump systems.

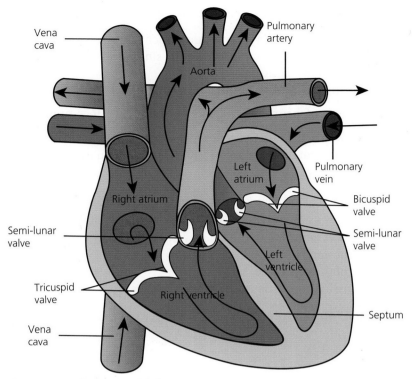

▲ Figure 1.4.4 The structure of the heart

There are many blood vessels associated with the heart. The inferior and superior venae cavae bring deoxygenated blood from the body to the right atrium. The pulmonary veins bring oxygenated blood from the lungs to the left atrium. The pulmonary artery takes deoxygenated blood from the right ventricle to the lungs. The aorta takes oxygenated blood from the left ventricle to the rest of the body.

Like other muscles the heart muscle (myocardium) requires a blood supply and this is transported to the heart muscle via the coronary artery giving oxygenated blood to the heart muscle via capillaries. Deoxygenated blood is taken away from the heart and into the right atrium through the coronary sinus.

The heart also consists of valves, which ensure that the blood can flow in one direction only. There are four valves within the heart: two that separate the atria from the ventricles and two in the arteries carrying blood from the ventricles. To stop the backflow of blood, the valves work one way only. The blood, which flows from the atria to the ventricles, pushes the valves open; the valves are then closed due to blood pressure.

Atrioventricular valves is a collective term for all the valves between atria and ventricles. The locations of the valves are as follows:

- **tricuspid valve**: valve between the right atrium and the right ventricle.
- **bicuspid valve**: valve between the left atrium and the left ventricle.
- **aortic valve**: valve between the left ventricle and the aorta.
- **pulmonary valve**: valve between the right ventricle and the pulmonary artery.
- **semilunar valves**: collective term for aortic and pulmonary valves.

> **STUDY HINT**
> The specification requires you to know the following structures and vessels associated with the heart. Make sure you know where they are and what they do:
> ✔ atria
> ✔ ventricles
> ✔ bicuspid, tricuspid and semilunar valves
> ✔ septum and major blood vessels:
>   ✓ aorta
>   ✓ pulmonary artery
>   ✓ vena cava
>   ✓ pulmonary vein.

> **STUDY HINT**
> Remember: the right-side pump sends deoxygenated blood to the lungs and the pump on the left-hand side sends oxygenated blood to the body's muscles.

Heart rate (HR)

The heart contracts and relaxes in a rhythm, which produces a heartbeat. This is started by an electrical impulse from the sino-atrial (SA) node, which is the 'pacemaker' of the heart.

Heart rate is measured by beats per minute. The average resting HR is 75 bpm.

$$\text{Measurement of heart rate} = \text{beats per minute (HR = bpm)}$$

A decrease in resting heart rate is a good indicator of fitness. A trained athlete's resting heart rate falls below 60 bpm. This is known as bradycardia.

Stroke volume (SV)

This is the volume of blood that is pumped out of the heart by each ventricle during one contraction. Stroke volume varies depending on the:

- amount of blood returning to the heart (venous return)
- elasticity of the ventricles
- contractility of the ventricles
- blood pressure in the arteries leading from the heart.

$$\text{Measurement of stroke volume (SV)} = \text{millilitres per beat (ml per beat)}$$

Cardiac output (Q)

This refers to the volume of blood ejected from the left ventricle in one minute. The cardiac output is equal to the stroke volume × the heart rate:

$$\text{Cardiac output (Q)} = \text{Stroke volume (SV)} \times \text{Heart rate (HR)}$$

$$\text{Measurement of Q} = \text{litres/min}$$

If an athlete's resting heart rate falls below 60 bpm, to produce the same cardiac output the stroke volume has to increase to compensate for the drop in heart rate. This is caused by an increase in the size of the heart (myocardial hypertrophy). The higher the cardiac output, the more oxygen can be delivered to the muscles and the longer and harder the athlete can work.

▲ Figure 1.4.5 The more oxygen can be delivered to the muscles, the longer and harder the athlete can work

❓ Extend your knowledge

Blood pressure (BP)

This is the force of blood applied to the blood vessel walls. It is the pressure needed to pump the blood around the body. It is measured by blood flow multiplied by the resistance to that flow. An instrument called a sphygmomanometer often takes blood pressure.

Measurement of blood pressure = millimetres of mercury (mmHg)

Systolic blood pressure is measured when the heart forcibly ejects blood. **Diastolic blood pressure** is measured when the heart relaxes.

The average blood pressure reading for an adult is 120/80 mmHg. The first number is the systolic blood pressure and the second number is the diastolic blood pressure. With regular exercise resting blood pressure can be reduced. For example, former British cyclist Chris Boardman said he had a resting heart rate of 38 bpm at his peak. He won three stages of the Tour de France during his career, sometimes cycling up to eight hours non-stop to train. Other factors affecting blood pressure are age, stress and diet.

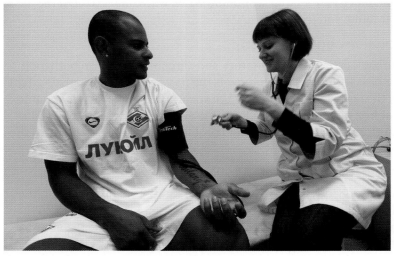

▲ Figure 1.4.6 With regular exercise resting BP can be reduced

Activity

Draw and label each type of blood vessel.
Write an account of the journey of blood from the heart and back to the heart. Describe what happens along this journey.

✔ Check your understanding

The cardiovascular system

1. Name the two elements of the double circulatory system.
2. What are the differences between arteries, capillaries and veins?
3. List the vessels showing the pathway of blood into and out of the heart.
4. What is meant by the following terms?
   - Heart rate
   - Stroke volume
   - Cardiac output
5. What is the main role of red blood cells?

Structure and function of the respiratory system

The respiratory system is important to study in combination with the cardiovascular system because the two systems work closely together to maintain a supply of oxygen to the working muscles, which is so crucial in sport. The external respiratory system involves the exchange of gases between the lungs and the blood. The internal respiratory system involves the exchange of gases between the blood and the cells.

The pathway of air through the respiratory system

Nasal passages

The air enters the body by being drawn in through the nose. The nasal cavity is divided by a cartilaginous septum that forms the nasal passages. Here the mucus membranes, or damp walls, warm and moisten the air and the hair filters and traps dust.

The pharynx and the larynx

The throat has both the respiratory and alimentary tract, so both food and air pass through. The pharynx is the passage to the digestive system and to the larynx. Air passes over the vocal cords of the larynx and into the **trachea** or windpipe. Swallowing draws the larynx upwards against the **epiglottis** and prevents the entry of food. Any food is sent down the oesophagus (foodpipe).

The bronchi and bronchioles

The trachea divides into two bronchi. The right bronchus goes into the right lung and the left bronchus goes into the left lung. The bronchi then divide up into smaller bronchioles. The bronchioles enable the air to pass into the alveoli, where gaseous exchange takes place.

Alveoli

These are responsible for gaseous exchange between the lungs and the blood. They are tiny air-filled sacs and there are millions of them in the lungs, providing an enormous surface area (estimated as the size of a tennis court). The walls of the alveoli are extremely thin and are lined by a thin film of water, which allows the dissolving of oxygen from air as it is breathed into the lungs (inspired).

Gaseous exchange

Within the alveoli, an exchange of gases takes place between the gases inside the alveoli and the blood.

Blood arriving in the alveoli has a higher carbon dioxide concentration, which is produced by the body's cells. The air in the alveoli has a much lower concentration of carbon dioxide, which allows carbon dioxide to diffuse from the blood and into the alveoli.

Blood arriving in the alveoli has a lower oxygen concentration (as it has been used for respiration by the body's cells), while the air in the alveoli has

Key terms

Trachea This is sometimes called the windpipe. It has 18 rings of cartilage, which are lined with a mucous membrane and ciliated cells, which trap dust. The trachea goes from the larynx to the primary bronchi.

Epiglottis The main function of this flap of tissue is to close over the windpipe (trachea) while you're eating, to prevent food entering your airways.

a higher oxygen concentration. Therefore, oxygen moves into the blood, again by diffusion, and combines with the haemoglobin in red blood cells to form **oxyhaemoglobin**.

Athletes who are involved with endurance events have a greater ability to diffuse oxygen because of an increase in cardiac output and in the surface area of the alveoli. The exchange of oxygen is illustrated in Figure 1.4.7.

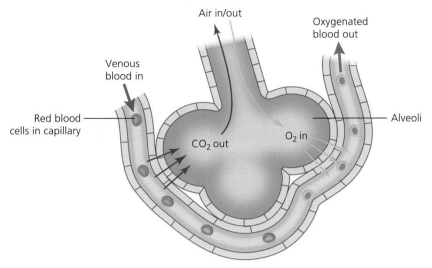

▲ Figure 1.4.7 Gaseous exchange at the alveoli

The role of respiratory muscles in breathing

Inspiration (breathing in)

The respiratory muscles contract. These include the external intercostal muscles and the diaphragm. The external intercostal muscles are attached to the ribs and when they contract, the ribs move upwards and outwards. The diaphragm contracts downwards and thus the area of the thoracic cavity is increased. The lungs are pulled outwards through surface tension along with the chest walls, which causes the space within the lungs to increase. The pressure within the lungs decreases and becomes less than the pressure outside the body. Gases move from areas of high pressure into areas of low pressure and so air is inspired into the lungs.

Expiration (breathing out)

This is more of a passive process than inspiration and is caused by the relaxation of the respiratory muscles. When the external intercostal muscles relax, the ribs are lowered and the diaphragm relaxes. The area of the lungs decreases and the pressure within the lungs becomes greater than the pressure outside the body. Air is now forced out to equalise this pressure and expiration takes place. The frequency of breathing is called the **breathing rate**.

Key terms

Oxyhaemoglobin Haemoglobin combines with oxygen in the lungs to form a bright red chemical called oxyhaemoglobin. When the blood gets to places where oxygen is being used up, oxyhaemoglobin releases the oxygen and turns back into haemoglobin.

Breathing rate Sometimes called the respiratory rate or ventilation rate, it is the frequency of breathing measured in breaths per minute. Normal breathing rate at rest is approximately 12 breaths per minute.

? Extend your knowledge

During exercise the sternocleidomastoid muscle lifts the sternum; the scalenes and the pectoralis minor both elevate the ribs. These actions help to increase the size of the thoracic cavity.

Key term

Lactic acid With the absence of oxygen, lactic acid is formed in the working muscles. Lactic acid causes muscle pain and fatigue. It often leads us to stop or reduce the activity we are doing.

Tidal volume

The volume of air that is inspired or expired per breath is known as tidal volume.

Minute ventilation

The volume of air that is inspired or expired in one minute is called minute ventilation. This is calculated by multiplying tidal volume by the number of breaths per minute:

$$VE = TV \times f$$

where VE is minute ventilation (l/min)
TV is tidal volume (ml)
f = number of breaths per minute.

✔ Check your understanding

Describe the structure and function of the respiratory system, the mechanisms of breathing, and respiratory volumes.
Explain the function of the respiratory system, including the mechanism of breathing.

Aerobic and anaerobic exercise

Many types of sports and exercise involve both aerobic and anaerobic aspects, but some are predominantly one or the other.

Aerobic exercise

Aerobic fitness is the ability to continuously exercise without tiring. The more oxygen that can be transported around the body and the more the muscles can utilise this oxygen determines the level of aerobic endurance you have. The level of endurance fitness is indicated by an individual's VO_2 max, which is the maximum amount of oxygen an individual can take in and use in one minute.

For most people, low to moderate exercise or exertion is generally aerobic. With aerobic exercise, oxygen is carried through your breath to the muscles, helping them to provide the energy needed to sustain effort. When we exercise aerobically our bodies use glycogen (carbohydrates) and fat as fuel. This low to moderate level of exertion (e.g. light jogging) can be sustained over long periods. As you breathe more heavily with exercise, carbon dioxide is expelled from your body. **Lactic acid** is not produced as it is with anaerobic exercise.

Activities that rely heavily on aerobic endurance are long-distance running in athletics, some activities in invasion games and outdoor activities such as hiking and rock climbing. Aerobic exercise also includes simply running at a comfortable pace (you should be able to talk comfortably while running), swimming and cycling.

Aerobic training should be carried out at a steady rate or with low intensity – between 20 minutes and 2 hours. This type of training ensures that there is not the build-up of lactate associated with anaerobic training.

Anaerobic exercise

Anaerobic fitness is being able to exercise without the use of oxygen; instead we use glycogen within the muscles as a fuel. Anaerobic energy produces short-term bursts of energy and does not require oxygen. During anaerobic exercise the body produces lactic acid. Anaerobic exercise is high intensity or at your maximum level of work. Examples include sprinting and weight lifting.

For training the anaerobic system, there should be shorter intervals of more intense training. The work interval should be up to 30 seconds at high intensity for anaerobic exercise.

The intensity of the work interval should be 90–100 per cent of maximum intensity for anaerobic exercise.

▲ Figure 1.4.8 Athletes rely on high levels of aerobic endurance

IN THE NEWS

HIIT

Recent trends in exercise and training include high-intensity interval training (HIIT).

Recent research has indicated that a key aspect in reducing the likelihood of early death from cardiovascular disease could be high-intensity exercise, although many in the medical establishment are still promoting moderate-intensity exercise.

Short bursts of activity, such as sprinting or pedalling all-out on an exercise bike for about 30 seconds, can result in the body getting rid of fat faster during recovery than exercising at moderate intensity, such as jogging. This type of exercise can reduce the chances of suffering a heart attack.

? Extend your knowledge

Anaerobic exercise helps build lean muscle mass. Anaerobic exercise is especially helpful for weight management in that it helps to burn more calories even in a body at rest. Anaerobic exercise can also help build endurance and fitness levels.

STUDY HINT

Differences between aerobic and anaerobic:

Aerobic	Anaerobic
Stimulates your heart rate and breathing to increase and you can sustain the activity for more than a few minutes	You get out of breath in just a few moments, such as when you lift weights for improving strength, when you sprint, or when you climb a long flight of stairs
With oxygen	Without oxygen
Low intensity with long duration	High intensity with short duration

SUMMARY

- Blood in the body continuously flows through a network of blood vessels that forms a double circuit. This circuit connects the heart to the lungs and then the heart to the other organs in the body. This double circuit involves pulmonary circulation and systemic circulation.
- Arteries are blood vessels that carry blood at high pressure from the heart to the body tissues.
- Veins carry blood at low pressure and return the blood to the heart.
- Capillaries have a single layer of cells in their walls and occur in large quantities around the muscles and this enables effective exchange of gases.
- Heart rate (HR) is measured by beats per minute (bpm). The average resting HR is 75 bpm.
- Stroke volume (SV) is the volume of blood that is pumped out of the heart by each ventricle during one contraction.
- Cardiac output (Q) refers to the volume of blood ejected from the left ventricle in one minute. The cardiac output is equal to the stroke volume × the heart rate.
- The primary function of red blood cells is to transport oxygen to cells around the body and to return carbon dioxide to the lungs.
- Gases move from areas of high pressure into areas of low pressure and so air is inspired into the lungs.
- Within the alveoli, an exchange of gases takes place between the gases inside the alveoli and the blood.
- Breathing rate is the frequency of breathing measured in breaths per minute.
- Tidal volume is the volume of air that is inspired or expired per breath.
- Minute ventilation is the volume of air that is inspired or expired in one minute.
- Aerobic exercise uses oxygen.
- Aerobic training should be carried out at a steady rate or at low intensity.
- Anaerobic fitness is being able to exercise without the use of oxygen.
- During anaerobic exercise the body produces lactic acid.

✔ Check your understanding

1. Which of the following activities would be best described as both aerobic *and* anaerobic?
   a. Sprinting
   b. Long jump
   c. Weight lifting
   d. Tennis

2. Natalie has decided to take up cross-country running. Which type of training would be most suitable for this activity?
   a. Circuit training
   b. Weight training
   c. Continuous training
   d. Flexibility training

3. Explain the difference between aerobic and anaerobic exercise.

Practice questions

1. Explain what is meant by the double circulatory system.
   (4 marks)

2. Describe the following blood vessels:
   - arteries
   - veins
   - capillaries.   **(3 marks)**

3. Define heart rate, stroke volume and cardiac output.
   (3 marks)

4. Outline the role of red blood cells.   **(3 marks)**

5. Describe the pathway of air through the respiratory system.   **(6 marks)**

6. Explain the process of gaseous exchange in the alveoli of the lungs.   **(5 marks)**

7. Using practical examples, explain what is meant by anaerobic exercise.   **(4 marks)**

Chapter 1.5
The effects of exercise on the body systems

Understanding the Specification

You should understand the short-term effects of exercise on the cardiovascular and muscular systems and be able to apply the effects to examples from physical activity/sport. You will need to collect and use data relating to short-term effects of exercise.

You should understand the long-term effects of exercise on bones, muscles and the cardiovascular system and be able to apply the effects to examples from physical activity/sport. You will be able to collect and use data relating to the long-term effects of exercise.

Short-term effects of exercise on the body systems

The following section looks at the short-term effects of exercise on the muscular, respiratory and cardiovascular systems. It's important that athletes have an understanding of this because they will be able to recognise their body's reaction to exercise and thus take suitable rests or identify areas of fitness they may need to improve.

Muscular system

The immediate effects of exercise on the muscular system involve an increase in the temperature of muscles and metabolic activity or **metabolism**. There is also an increase in the production of lactic acid in the muscles depending on the type of exercise. This increase in the production of lactic acid is a result of prolonged high-intensity exercise when there is a lack of oxygen in the muscles.

Effects of lactic acid

Lactic acid produced in the muscles results in muscular pain and fatigue and often leads to the activity being stopped or curtailed. Therefore the build-up of lactic acid has a negative effect on our ability to keep exercising. During recovery, the intake of oxygen helps to convert lactic acid into waste products such as water and carbon dioxide (CO_2).

Key term

Metabolism This involves the many continuous chemical processes inside the body that are essential for living, moving and growing. The number of kilojoules the body burns is regulated by the rate of metabolism.

> ### ❓ Extend your knowledge
>
> The two main processes that make up metabolism are the breakdown of food to give energy, called catabolism, and the building and repair of muscle tissue, called anabolism. The amount of metabolism that takes place is called the metabolic rate. Strength training can offset the effects of ageing and helps to retain muscle mass.
>
> The increase in metabolic activity means that the body needs more oxygen and this results in the capillaries within the muscles getting wider or dilating. It is often thought that the warming of muscle fibres can make them more flexible and therefore injuries such as strains are less likely to occur. The opposite can also occur – for example, a short-term effect of exercise on muscles can be to induce injury and pain might be experienced.

The cardiovascular system

In the short term, the heart rate is raised just before exercise and will increase during exercise to ensure that there is enough supply of oxygen to the working muscles and that waste products, such as carbon dioxide, are removed. The raising of the heart rate before exercise is called the **anticipatory rise**.

▲ Figure 1.5.1 When the heart rate rises before exercise, this is called the anticipatory rise

When exercise begins the heart rate will rise rapidly. As exercise continues, the heart muscle also becomes warmer. When exercise ceases, the heart rate will fall rapidly and the level of **adrenaline** falls, along with a drop in temperature of the heart. The heart rate then returns to around its pre-exercise rate. During exercise, the working skeletal muscles require more and more oxygen. The increase in stroke volume, cardiac output and heart rate enables more oxygen to be delivered, but this is often not enough and therefore the **vascular shunt** mechanism takes effect.

> **STUDY HINT**
> The main effect of exercise on the cardiovascular system is an increase in:
> ✔ heart rate (beats per minute)
> ✔ stroke volume (the volume of blood that is pumped out of the heart by each ventricle during one contraction)
> ✔ cardiac output (the volume of blood ejected from the left ventricle in one minute. The cardiac output is equal to the stroke volume × the heart rate).

The respiratory system

The short-term response of the respiratory system to exercise includes a rise in the respiratory rate (breathing rate) due to the body's demands for more oxygen.

Tidal volume (TV) also increases during exercise. This is the volume of air either inspired or expired per breath.

Minute ventilation also increases during exercise. This is the volume of air that is inspired and expired in one minute.

Key terms

Anticipatory rise This is the raising of the heart rate before exercise begins. It is caused through the release of adrenaline, which is a hormone.

Adrenaline This is a hormone released from the adrenal glands and its major action is to prepare the body for 'fight or flight'.

Vascular shunts occur when more blood is distributed to the working muscles and less to the non-essential organs. The vascular shunt mechanism involves two processes:

- The arterioles (smaller arteries) that supply muscle tissue experience vasodilation (diameter increases) and this increases the blood flow to the muscles. Vasoconstriction (diameter decreases) of the arterioles that supply other organs such as the liver means that blood flow is lessened to these organs that do not require as much blood supply.

- In the capillaries that supply the skeletal muscles the precapillary sphincters (valves) open up and blood flow is again increased. In the capillaries that supply other organs, the precapillary sphincters close, thus decreasing the blood flow.

The result of these processes is to significantly increase the supply of oxygen to the working muscles during exercise.

❓ Extend your knowledge

- Inspiratory reserve volume (IRV) – this is the maximal volume inspired in addition to the tidal volume. This decreases during exercise
- Expiratory reserve volume (ERV) – this is the maximal volume expired in addition to the tidal volume. This decreases slightly during exercise.
- Reserve or residual volume (RV) – this is the amount of air left in the lungs after maximal expiration. This increases slightly during exercise.
- Vital capacity (VC) – this is the maximum amount of air that can be forcibly exhaled after maximal inspiration. This decreases slightly during exercise.
- Total lung capacity (TLC) – this is the vital capacity plus the reserve or residual volume and is the volume at the end of maximal inspiration. This decreases slightly during exercise.

Activity

Collecting and using data relating to short-term effects of exercise

Analyse how the cardiovascular system responds to exercise.
- Record your resting pulse rate.
- Using a treadmill or an exercise bike, cycle with moderate effort for 20 minutes.
- Record your pulse rate every four minutes and then finally at the end.
- Then record your pulse rate after every four minutes once you have finished.
- Record how you feel before the exercise and then after the 20 minutes are up.
- Draw a graph showing your pulse rate before, during and after exercise.

Describe what has happened to the cardiovascular system during your ride.

Explain these effects – e.g. why has your heart rate increased just before exercise? How do you account for any changes in your feelings?

Analyse the possible long-term effects of exercise on the cardiovascular system if you continued with this training three times a week, increasing the effort over a period of eight weeks.

Long-term effects of exercise on the body systems

This section explores the long-term effects of exercise on these systems. It's important that athletes have an understanding of both the short-term and the long-term effects, so that they can identify which areas require improvement and are aware of their body's reactions to exercise.

Muscular system

The long-term responses to exercise of the muscular system depend on the amount and the intensity of the exercise undertaken. Muscular strength and muscle size can increase with a programme of weight or resistance (against weights or body weight) training.

▲ Figure 1.5.2 Muscular strength and muscle size can increase with a programme of weight or resistance training.

Following resistance training, there is an increase in the thickness of the muscle fibres due to greater muscle protein. Muscle strength will therefore be increased along with strength of **tendons**.

Following flexibility training, there is often an increase in the range of movement possible around a joint.

Following endurance (stamina) training, **muscular endurance** increases. The slow twitch (concerned with stamina activities) muscle fibres will get larger by up to around 20 per cent. This means that there is greater potential for energy production. Endurance training will also increase the capacity to carry oxygen and the athlete will become aerobically fitter.

Following training of high intensity, often called anaerobic training, the fast twitch fibres will increase in size – this is called **hypertrophy**. Muscles will also be able to work for longer and the athlete's muscle fatigue or tiredness will be delayed following this type of training.

IN THE NEWS

Effects of exercise on the muscular system – practical example

The coach of a football striker was concerned that the player was not jumping high enough in the air to win the high ball against defenders. The player, although skilful on the ground, kept losing out on corners and high crosses. The coach constructed a training regime to improve the player's leg strength. Having followed a pre-season six-week programme, the striker's performance improved and he was more able to compete effectively for the high ball against defenders. The player also worked on his flexibility and reported that the range of movement around his hips had improved and he felt that his leg muscles were more toned.

Key terms

Tendons Muscles are attached to bones by tendons. These tendons help to 'pull' the muscle to the bone and help with the power of muscle contractions. Tendons are attached to the periosteum (a membrane that covers the outer surface of bones) of the bone through tough tissue called Sharpey's fibres.

Muscular endurance This is the ability of the muscle or group of muscles to repeatedly contract or keep going without rest.

Hypertrophy This term means that there is an increase in the size or the mass of an organ in the body or a muscle. Hypertrophy often occurs as a result of regular training or exercise and can lead to an increase in muscular strength and power.

Activity

1. What are the possible reasons for the training improving the player's jumping ability?
2. Why have flexibility and tone also improved?
3. What activities would you have included in the leg strength training?

> **Activity**
>
> Using the information from this chapter, briefly list the short-term and the long-term effects of exercise on the muscular system.
>
> Now give reasons for why these responses or adaptations have taken place.

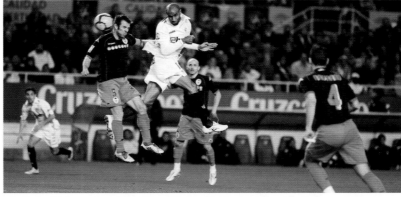

▲ Figure 1.5.3 Leg strength training will help with jumping to head the ball

The cardiovascular system

The long-term effects of exercise and training depend on the duration and intensity of the training, but with most training programmes the heart will become stronger and will increase in size. This increase in size is known as cardiac hypertrophy. This will occur particularly with endurance-type exercise or training. The wall of the left ventricle becomes thicker, thus increasing the strength of contractions in the heart. This increase in contractions will ensure more blood is delivered to the working muscles. More blood is pumped from the heart per beat of the heart and therefore stroke volume will increase. Cardiac output will also therefore increase during high or maximal levels of exercise.

The resting heart rate will also fall as a long-term consequence of exercise and training. This reduces how hard the heart needs to work and the heart rate returns to normal more quickly following exercise. Resting stroke volume also increases. When the resting heart rate falls below 60 beats per minute this is known as bradycardia.

> **STUDY HINT**
>
> The vascular shunt mechanism is important because during exercise, the working skeletal muscles require more and more oxygen. The increase in stroke volume and heart rate enables more oxygen to be delivered, but this is not enough.

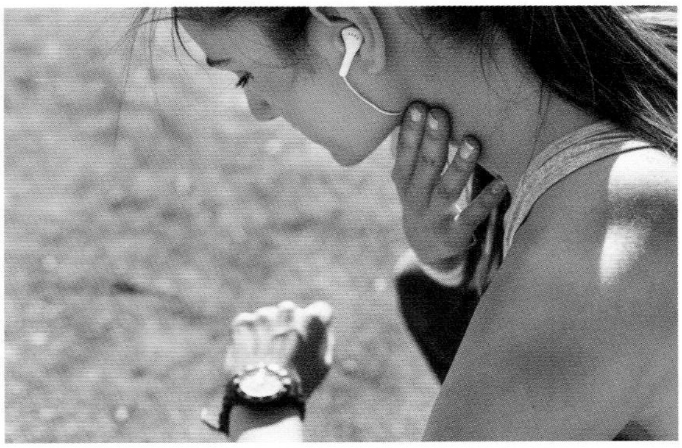

▲ Figure 1.5.4 The effect of endurance training is to lower the resting heart rate.

Other long-term effects of exercise on the cardiovascular system include the following:

- There is increased capillarisation of muscles, meaning new capillaries may develop. This enables more blood to flow and therefore more oxygen to reach the muscle tissues. Existing capillaries also become more efficient with similar effects.
- Blood vessels become more efficient with the vascular shunt mechanism.

> **Activity**
>
> The Tour de France cyclist Miguel Indurain is known to have a resting pulse rate of 30 beats per minute.
>
> 1. What has caused bradycardia in this cyclist?
> 2. How does the cyclist's cardiovascular system adapt in the short term just before and just after the race has begun?
> 3. Other than bradycardia, name one other long term effect of exercise on the cardiovascular system of such a cyclist.

- Blood pressure, if previously high, decreases at rest. This is because the cardiovascular system has become more efficient.
- There is an increase in the number of red blood cells. This will also mean that haemoglobin content is higher and therefore more oxygen can be delivered to muscles.
- There is a decrease in **blood viscosity** that again makes oxygen carriage more effective and can reduce blood pressure.

Key term

Blood viscosity This refers to the thickness of the blood and how resistant the blood is to flow freely. The more viscous the blood, the more it resists free flow. The amount of plasma or water content of the blood affects the viscosity. Therefore to ensure fast blood flow the plasma level needs also to be high.

✔ Check your knowledge

- Describe how the cardiovascular system responds to exercise.
- Explain the function of the cardiovascular system and how it responds to exercise.

The respiratory system

The long-term effects of exercise, or adaptations, on the respiratory system are as follows:

- There is an increase in capillary density, which increases the efficiency of oxygen uptake for energy.
- There is a slight increase in vital capacity, which means more air can be inspired, and also a slight increase in tidal volume, which means again more oxygen can enter the lungs.
- There is greater intercostal muscle strength, allowing more air to be breathed in and out, and a reduction in resting respiratory rate, which makes the body more efficient.
- The exchange of gases at the alveoli (pulmonary diffusion) becomes more efficient and therefore the body can work harder and longer due to the increased surface area of the alveoli. An increase in capillarisation again leads to more effective uptake of oxygen and more effective removal of carbon dioxide.

✔ Check your knowledge

A student who recently joined a rugby club has started to train twice a week. Training involves stamina or endurance running. Immediately after the training session the student's breathing is very rapid. After about eight weeks, she is less out of breath after training and on match days she seems to be able to keep running for longer without getting out of breath.

Questions

1. Why does the student get out of breath immediately after training?
2. What other short-term effects might there be related to the respiratory system?
3. Why is she now less out of breath during a rugby match?

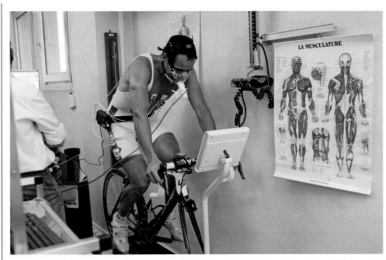

▲ Figure 1.5.5 Training and regular exercise can ensure long-term adaptations of the respiratory system

Activity

Draw out the grid shown below. In the first column name both the short-term and the long-term adaptations of the respiratory system as a result of exercise. In the second column analyse these effects by explaining what happens as a result of these adaptations.

	Adaptations	Effects of these adaptations on the body
Short-term effects of exercise on the respiratory system		
Long-term effects of exercise on the respiratory system		

Other long-term effects of exercise

In the longer term, and with more persistent exercise, the connective tissue around the skeleton becomes more flexible. Over a period of time the short-term improvement in the range of movement becomes more sustained. Skeletal bone increases in its density as a result of exercise. This makes the bones stronger and can help to offset the effects of bone disease such as **osteoporosis**.

Hyaline cartilage also thickens with exercise, which helps to cushion the joint, therefore preventing damage to the bone. Tendons thicken and the ligaments have a greater stretch potential, again helping to protect the body from injury. The bone mineral content of calcium and phosphate has been shown to be significantly higher in those that participate in regular exercise for all ages than those who do not. This is a compelling reason for regular exercise for all, including the elderly.

Key term

Osteoporosis This is a disease in which bones become fragile and more likely to break. If not prevented or if left untreated, osteoporosis can progress painlessly until a bone breaks. These broken bones, also known as fractures, occur typically in the hip, spine and wrist.

Activity

Collecting and using data relating to long-term effects of exercise

- Before an exercise programme, carry out a cardiovascular endurance test, such as the bleep test, and a flexibility test, such as the sit and reach test.
- Record your results (data).
- Follow a training programme for 6–8 weeks, such as the training described in the earlier activity related to short-term effects. You should train three times a week and increase the intensity over a period of eight weeks.
- Repeat the tests and record your results in a data table.
- Draw graphs to show the changes in scores for cardiovascular endurance and flexibility.
- Using your results data and the graphs you have drawn, analyse the possible long-term effects of exercise on the cardiovascular system if you continued with the training described.

❓ Extend your knowledge

Osteoporosis occurs when the body may fail to form enough new bone, or too much old bone may be reabsorbed, or both. Two essential minerals for normal bone formation are calcium and phosphate.

The leading cause of osteoporosis is a lack of certain hormones, particularly oestrogen in women. Women, especially those older than 60 years, are frequently diagnosed with the disease. Other factors that may contribute to bone loss in this age group include inadequate intake of calcium and vitamin D and a lack of weight-bearing exercise.

SUMMARY

- The immediate effects of exercise on the muscular system involve an increase in the temperature of muscles and metabolic activity or metabolism.
- In the short term, the heart rate is raised just before exercise and will increase during exercise to ensure that there is enough supply of oxygen to the working muscles.
- The increase in the heart rate before exercise is called the anticipatory rise.
- The short-term response of the respiratory system to exercise includes a rise in the respiratory rate (breathing rate) due to the body's demands for more oxygen.
- Tidal volume (TV) also increases during exercise. This is the volume of air either inspired or expired per breath.
- Minute ventilation also increases during exercise. This is the volume of air that is inspired and expired in one minute.
- The long-term responses to exercise of the muscular system depend on the amount and the intensity of the exercise.
- Following resistance training, there is an increase in the thickness of the muscle fibres due to greater muscle protein.
- Endurance training will also increase the capacity to take in, carry and use oxygen and the athlete will become aerobically fitter.
- The long-term effects of exercise and training depend on the duration and intensity of the training.
- Skeletal bone increases in its density as a result of exercise. This makes the bones stronger and can help to offset the effects of bone disease such as osteoporosis.

✔ Check your understanding

1. What are the short- and long-term effects of exercise on the cardiovascular system?
2. What are the short- and long-term effects of exercise on the muscular system?
3. What are the short- and long-term effects of exercise on the respiratory system?
4. What happens to bones after a long-term training programme?
5. What is meant by hypertrophy?

Practice questions

1. Describe the short-term effects of exercise on the heart.
    (4 marks)
2. Outline the redistribution of blood during exercise.
    (3 marks)
3. Why is lactic acid produced? **(3 marks)**
4. What is the long-term effect of exercise on bones? **(1 mark)**
5. Describe the long-term effects of exercise on the muscular system. **(4 marks)**
6. Explain what is meant by hypertrophy of the heart and muscles. **(2 marks)**
7. The graph below shows the difference between the heart rate of a fit person who exercises regularly and someone who does not exercise. Explain these differences between the two people. **(4 marks)**

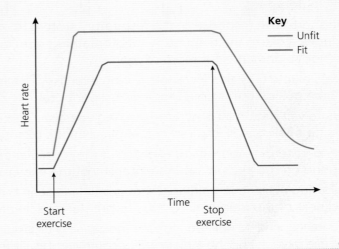

Section 2
Physical Training

2.1 Components of fitness
2.2 Applying the principles of training
2.3 Preventing injury in physical activity
and training

Chapter 2.1
Components of fitness

Understanding the Specification

On completion of this topic you should know the definition of each of the following components of fitness, know a suitable test for each component and be able to give practical examples where each component is particularly important:

- cardiovascular endurance/stamina
- muscular endurance
- speed
- strength
- power
- flexibility
- agility
- balance
- co-ordination
- reaction time.

You should also be able to collect and use data relating to the components of fitness.

Fitness can be seen as a group of components that if trained will enable the body to do more work and for longer, as well as be more skilful in sports activities. Fitness is often referred to as one aspect. However, it is not and different components of fitness need to be trained for different types of activities. For example, if you were to run a marathon, although all aspects of fitness are important you would probably work more on your cardiovascular endurance fitness. If you are a gymnast then you might work more on your strength and flexibility.

Cardiovascular endurance/ stamina

Key term

VO$_2$ max The maximum amount of oxygen an individual can take in and use in one minute.

This is sometimes called aerobic endurance. Cardiovascular endurance is the ability to continuously exercise without tiring. The more oxygen that can be transported around the body and the more the muscles can utilise or use this oxygen, the more cardiovascular endurance you have. The level of endurance fitness is indicated by an individual's **VO$_2$ max**.

The body adapts to endurance training and aerobic adaptations occur. The more aerobic endurance you have, the more the onset of fatigue can be delayed, or in other words the less tired you get. High levels of cardiovascular endurance can ensure that the body has the ability to exercise whole muscle groups over an extended period of time at moderate intensity, using or utilising aerobic energy. Your aerobic system uses oxygen to break down carbohydrates and convert them into energy that lasts.

Activities that rely heavily on cardiovascular endurance are long-distance running in athletics, invasion games and outdoor activities.

▲ Figure 2.1.1 Athletes such as long-distance swimmers rely on high levels of cardiovascular endurance

The cardiovascular system involves transporting oxygen around the body. The cardiovascular system includes:

- the heart
- the network of blood vessels
- the blood that transports essential material around the body.

Examples of activities where cardiovascular endurance is particularly important:

- Running
- Aerobics
- Swimming
- Fast walking
- Cross-country skiing
- Treadmill 15–20 min – light jog to run
- Cardio bike 15–20 min – medium to quick pace
- Skipping rope 10–15 min – fast pace.

Suitable tests for cardiovascular endurance

The level of endurance fitness is indicated by an individual's VO_2 max (that is, the maximum amount of oxygen an individual can take in and utilise in one minute). The potential VO_2 max of an individual can be predicted via tests such as the Cooper 12-minute run/walk test and the multistage fitness test.

Cooper 12-minute run/walk test

The 12-minute run/walk fitness test was developed from the work of Dr Ken Cooper in 1968 as a simple method to measure aerobic endurance and provide an estimate of VO_2 max. Dr Cooper found that there was a very high correlation or relationship between the distance someone could run or walk in 12 minutes and their VO_2 max, which measures the efficiency with which someone can use oxygen while exercising.

Walking

Some volunteers were asked to complete three 50-minute sessions a week of moderate physical activity, such as walking, for 24 weeks. Others were asked not to increase their exercise levels.

At the end of the study, the people in the exercise group achieved better scores in tests of their cognitive function and lower scores in tests to determine signs of dementia. Follow-up showed that the benefits persisted for at least another 12 months after the exercise programme was stopped. Exercise is known to help keep the cardiovascular system healthy and may help boost cognitive function by boosting blood supply to the brain.

IN THE NEWS

Cardiovascular exercise may help improve mental performance in adults

A University of Melbourne team in 2008 tested the impact of a home-based physical activity programme on 138 volunteers aged 50 and over with memory problems. Those who took part showed a modest improvement in cognitive function (thinking skills) compared with those who did not.

The Journal of the American Medical Association study suggests exercise may help ward off severe mental decline.

Dementia is already a serious problem and the number of people with Alzheimer's disease, the most common form of the condition, is predicted to quadruple worldwide over the next half century.

The latest study focused on people with mild cognitive (thought processes) impairment, a term used to describe memory problems that are not serious enough to interfere with everyday life. It does not necessarily lead to dementia, but it does increase the risk of developing the condition.

The Cooper 12-minute run/walk test requires the person being tested to run or walk as far as possible in a 12-minute period. The objective is to measure the maximum distance they can cover during 12 minutes. The test is usually carried out on a running track by placing cones at various points to measure the distance. A stopwatch is required to ensure the individual runs for the correct length of time.

Safety

This can be a strenuous fitness test and you should have your doctor's permission to carry it out, particularly if you have any underlying medical conditions such as asthma.

The test

- Perform a short 10–15 minute warm-up before performing the test.
- When you are warmed up, run or walk as far as you can in 12 minutes.
- Record the total number of metres you have travelled in 12 minutes.

To calculate your estimated VO_2 max results (in ml/kg/min) use either of these formulas:

- In miles: $VO_2max = (35.97 \times miles) - 11.29$.
- In kilometres: $VO_2max = (22.351 \times kilometres) - 11.288$

Compare your 12-minute run fitness test results

After you complete the test, you can compare your results to the norms and recommendations for your age and gender in Table 2.1.1. The norms are based on 20–29 year olds, but these will give you some idea of your own level of cardiovascular fitness. The distance in Table 2.1.1 is measured in metres.

▼ Table 2.1.1 12-minute run fitness test results interpretation

	Excellent	Above average	Average	Below average	Poor
Male 20–29	>2,800 m	2,400–2,800 m	2,200–2,399 m	1,600–2,199 m	<1,600 m
Females 20–29	>2,700 m	2,200–2,700 m	1,800–2,199 m	1,500–1,799 m	<1,500 m

Multistage fitness test

Sometimes called the 'bleep' or 'beep' test, this test involves a shuttle run that gets progressively more difficult. The test is published by what was the National Coaching Foundation and is in the form of a CD (there are now mobile phone apps that do a similar thing).

The test

Subjects are required to run a 20-metre shuttle as many times as possible but ensuring that they turn at each end of the run in time with the 'bleep' on the CD. The time lapse between each bleep sound on the CD gets progressively shorter and so the shuttle run has to be completed progressively quicker. At the point when the subject cannot keep up with the bleeps, they are deemed to have reached their optimum level. That level is recorded and used as a baseline for future tests or can be compared with national norms.

Safety

- A person experiencing shortness of breath, chest pains, palpitations or light-headedness should stop exercising immediately and be sensitively advised to seek advice from a general practitioner.
- Teachers or coaches should observe participants continuously while the test is taking place, keeping a particular eye on pupils known to be physically less fit.

Table 2.1.2 shows national team scores on the multistage fitness test.

▼ Table 2.1.2 National team scores on the multistage fitness test

Sport	Male	Female
Basketball	L11–S5	L9–S6
Hockey	L13–S9	L12–S7
Rugby League	L13–S1	
Netball		L9–S7
Squash	L13–S13	

L = level, S = shuttle

The multistage fitness test includes predictions of VO_2 max for individuals. Tables 2.1.3 and 2.1.4 outline norms for VO_2 max for different age groups.

▼ Table 2.1.3 Maximal oxygen uptake norms for men (ml/kg/min)

	18–25 years old	26–35 years old	36–45 years old	46–55 years old	56–65 years old	65+ years old
Excellent	>60	>56	>51	>45	>41	>37
Good	52–60	49–56	43–51	39–45	36–41	33–37
Above average	47–51	43–48	39–42	35–38	32–35	29–32
Average	42–46	40–42	35–38	32–35	30–31	26–28
Below average	37–41	35–39	31–34	29–31	26–29	22–25
Poor	30–36	30–34	26–30	25–28	22–25	20–21
Very poor	<30	<30	<26	<25	<22	<20

▼ Table 2.1.4 Maximal oxygen uptake norms for women (ml/kg/min)

	18–25 years old	26–35 years old	36–45 years old	46–55 years old	56–65 years old	65+ years old
Excellent	>60	>56	>51	>45	>41	>37
Good	52–60	49–56	43–51	39–45	36–41	33–37
Above average	47–51	43–48	39–42	35–38	32–35	29–32
Average	42–46	40–42	35–38	32–35	30–31	26–28
Below average	37–41	35–39	31–34	29–31	26–29	22–25
Poor	30–36	30–34	26–30	25–28	22–25	20–21
Very poor	<30	<30	<26	<25	<22	<20

STUDY HINT

Make sure you:
✔ learn the definition of cardiovascular endurance or stamina
✔ have clear practical examples of activities that are predominantly aerobic
✔ know the two tests for cardiovascular (VO_2) fitness.

IN THE NEWS

Multistage fitness test results for elite performers

Professional rugby flankers mostly score in the 12–13 range and prop forwards score around level 10. For females, the UK national women's rugby team averaged over 11, with a range from 9 to 12.

Muscular endurance

This is the ability of the muscle or group of muscles in the body to repeatedly contract or keep going without rest. For example, the number of press-ups you can perform depends on the muscular endurance of your pectorals, deltoids and triceps. You can target one or a few muscle groups when building muscular endurance, and you can build endurance using weight training or your body's resistance.

With a healthy, balanced lifestyle the muscular system can keep going because of greater aerobic potential. Activities such as swimming or running can enlarge slow twitch fibres, which gives greater potential for energy production. The onset of fatigue is delayed (you get tired less quickly) because of higher maximum oxygen uptake (VO₂ max).

With a healthy lifestyle muscles can keep going during repetitive tasks that are found in work and in sport and exercise, for example finishing an exercise routine or keeping up with your friends when walking home from school. By exercising, the size and number of **mitochondria** in muscles are increased. Also with exercise there is an increase in **myoglobin** content within the muscle cell.

Activities such as sprinting or weight lifting can cause hypertrophy or the build-up of **fast twitch muscle fibres**.

▲ Figure 2.1.2 Muscular endurance in the shoulders is very important to the canoeist

Examples of activities where muscular endurance is particularly important:

- Cross country running
- Cycling
- Swimming
- Rugby, football and hockey
- Step machine 15–20 min – quick pace
- Tuck jumps 15–25 reps

Suitable tests for muscular endurance

Testing the endurance of one particular muscle group can assess an individual's muscular endurance.

The press-up test

- Lie on the mat, hands shoulder width apart, and fully extend the arms.
- Lower the body until the elbows reach 90°.
- Return to the starting position with the arms fully extended.
- Do not hold the feet.
- Make the push-up action continuous, with no rest.
- Complete as many press-ups as possible.
- Record the total number of full-body press-ups.

Key terms

Mitochondria These are parts of each muscle cell and places where energy is produced – sometimes referred to as 'powerhouses' of muscle cells. Those who exercise regularly and participate in endurance activities such as long-distance cycling often have more mitochondria.

Myoglobin This is related to haemoglobin and is found in muscle cells that transport oxygen to the mitochondria to provide energy. Those who are more active – especially those who exercise regularly for endurance events such as marathon running – have higher levels of myoglobin.

Fast twitch muscle fibres Sometimes called Type II fibres. These are used to generate short bursts of speed or strength but these fibres fatigue very quickly.

Female athletes can use the modified press-up position to assess their upper body strength. The test is then performed as follows:

- Lie on the mat, hands shoulder width apart, bent knee position, and fully extend the arms.
- Lower the upper body until the elbows reach 90°.
- Return to the starting position with the arms fully extended.
- Do not hold the feet.
- Make the push-up action continuous, with no rest.
- Complete as many modified press-ups as possible.
- Record the total number of modified press-ups.

▲ Figure 2.1.3 Female athletes can use the modified press-up position to assess their upper body strength

▼ Normative data for the press-up tests

▼ Table 2.1.5 Full-body press-up

Age	Excellent	Good	Average	Fair	Poor
20–29	>54	45–54	35–44	20–34	<20
30–39	>44	35–44	25–34	15–24	<15
40–49	>39	30–39	20–29	12–19	<12
50–59	>34	25–34	15–24	8–14	<8
60+	>29	20–29	10–19	5–9	<5

▼ Table 2.1.6 Modified press-ups

Age	Excellent	Good	Average	Fair	Poor
20–29	>48	34–38	17–33	6–16	<6
30–39	>39	25–39	12–24	4–11	<4
40–49	>34	20–34	8–19	3–7	<3
50–59	>29	15–29	6–14	2–5	<2
60+	>19	5–19	3–4	1–2	<1

This test is easy, quick to perform and requires no equipment. The subject's motivation level rather than their fitness can be the deciding factor. Poor technique can also invalidate the results and could lead to injury.

The sit-up test

This tests the endurance of the abdominal muscle group by measuring the number of sit-ups (curl-ups) an individual can perform by keeping to a 'bleep' indicated on the recording/app. When the individual cannot complete any more sit-ups in time with the bleep, they are deemed to have reached their optimum level. Again this test can be used as a benchmark for training or used for comparison with national norms.

If you are suffering from any injury or illness, you should consult a doctor before doing this test.

▼ Table 2.1.7 Normative scores

Stage	Number of sit-ups cumulative	Standard male	Standard female
1	20	Poor	Poor
2	42	Poor	Fair
3	64	Fair	Fair
4	89	Fair	Good
5	116	Good	Good
6	146	Good	Very good
7	180	Excellent	Excellent
8	217	Excellent	Excellent

The test must be conducted by using the standardised instructions. The individual's level of motivation to perform the test can affect the results. This test is simple and quick to perform, requiring minimal equipment, and large groups may be tested at once.

The subject's technique can affect the results, e.g. a curl-up with the feet held increases the involvement of the hip flexor muscles, making the test less valid as a measure of abdominal strength.

Speed

This is the ability of the body to move quickly. The movements may be the whole body or parts of the body, for example arm speed in cricket bowling. Speed can be seen as the maximum rate that a person can move over a specific distance or speed of specific body parts such as the legs. Genetics influence how quick you are, but training can improve your rate or speed of movement. The amount of fast twitch muscle fibres also influences speed. Examples of activities where speed is particularly important include:

- athletics
- swimming
- squash
- games such as netball, football and basketball.

STUDY HINT

It is important that you can:
- ✔ define muscular endurance
- ✔ name activities that predominantly use muscular endurance
- ✔ describe the tests for muscular endurance.

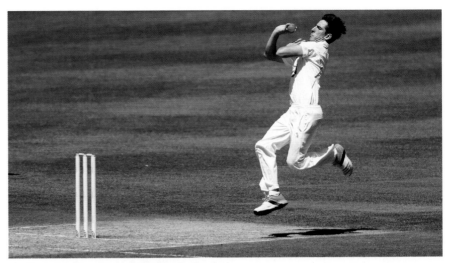

▲ Figure 2.1.4 Speed is important for a fast bowler

If you are fit and healthy your speed is helped because:

- your heart and lungs are more efficient
- your muscles can move quicker because they have more energy available
- the energy available is greater because your muscles are more efficient in producing energy
- your joints are more healthy and therefore they can help you to move more effectively.

Suitable test for speed

The 30-metre sprint test

This should be on a flat, non-slippery surface to prevent accidents. The sprint should be from a flying start back from the beginning of the marked-out stretch of running surface. The time is taken from the beginning of the 30m stretch to the end.

Before you do the test, you should have an appropriate warm-up and a practice sprint, You should be given some encouragement to continue running hard through the finish line (but this encouragement should be standardised to ensure validity).

Approximate norms for intermediate-level team players (30 m sprints) are shown in Table 2.1.8.

▼ Table 2.1.8 Approximate norms for 30 m sprints

Rating	Male	Female
Very good	<4.80 secs	<5.30 secs
Good	4.80–5.09	5.30–5.59
Average	5.10–5.29	5.60–5.89
Fair	5.30–5.60	5.90–6.20
Poor	>5.60	>6.20

▲ Figure 2.1.5 Speed is important in a lot of different sports activities

The test is easy to administer and no specialist equipment is required. However, the conditions must remain similar for each test. The appropriate warm-up should also be replicated. Sprint technique may affect times and the level of motivation may invalidate results. The timing procedure should be standardised and this is probably the weakest part of the test. The timer should be the same person for each subject's test. Timing can be unreliable and the activity could be dangerous without appropriate warm-up and if the surface is slippery. It is important for subjects to have appropriate footwear to avoid injury. Weather conditions can also affect the results if the test takes place outdoors.

Strength

This is the ability of a muscle to exert force for a short period of time. The amount of force that can be exerted by a muscle depends on the size and number of muscles involved, as well as the type of muscle fibres used and the co-ordination of the muscles. Sports such as cycling can enlarge **slow twitch fibres**, thus giving greater potential for energy production. When training for an increase in speed, the size and number of mitochondria increases, as does the myoglobin content in the muscle cells. There are **anaerobic** benefits to muscle with activities like sprinting because the muscles get bigger and stronger (hypertrophy).

Examples of activities where strength is particularly important:

- Sprinting
- Games activities such as rugby and American football
- Cycling
- Rowing

Suitable tests for strength

The grip strength dynamometer test

This test is an objective measure of strength using the handgrip dynamometer, which measures the strength of the handgrip. It is generally accepted that there is a strong correlation or link between handgrip strength and overall strength.

Key term

Slow twitch fibres (sometimes called type 1 muscle fibres) These are muscle fibres that can produce energy over a long period of time. They have high levels of myoglobin and mitochondria and are used for mainly aerobic activities.

Anaerobic This is when the body is working without the presence of oxygen, for example lifting something quickly off the floor or doing an activity such as sprinting for a ball. This type of activity can be carried out only for a short amount of time because of the lack of oxygen and the build-up of lactic acid.

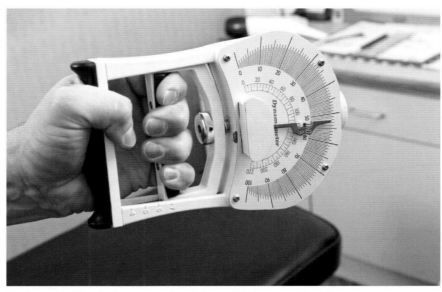

▲ Figure 2.1.6 The grip dynamometer is an instrument that measures strength

Make sure that the handgrip is adjusted to fit the subject's hand. The subject should stand, holding the dynamometer parallel to the side of the body, with the dial facing away from the body. They should squeeze the handle as hard as possible without moving the arm. Three attempts are recommended, with a one-minute rest between each attempt.
Table 2.1.9 outlines national norms for 16–19 year olds, showing the average from the three attempts with the favoured hand.

▼ Table 2.1.9 National norms for grip strength (favoured hand) for 16–19 year olds

Gender	Excellent	Good	Average	Fair	Poor
Male	>56 kg	51–56	45–50	39–44	<39
Female	>36 kg	31–36	25–30	19–24	<19

Another method of scoring is by recording the better of two attempts for each hand. Table 2.1.10 shows the average of the best scores of each hand (norms are in kilograms for adults).

▼ Table 2.1.10 National norms for grip strength (average of both hands) for 16–19 year olds

Rating*	Males (kg)	Females (kg)
Excellent	>64	>38
Very good	56–64	34–38
Above average	52–56	30–34
Average	48–52	26–30
Below average	44–48	22–26
Poor	40–44	20–22
Very poor	<40	<20

The validity of this test as a measure of general strength has been questioned, as the strength of the forearm muscles does not necessarily always represent the strength of other muscle groups.

This is a simple and easily used test indicating general strength level. It is relatively safe and quick to administer. There is no need for specific facilities – the only equipment required is the dynamometer. However, the dynamometer must be adjusted properly for the athlete's hand size; if this is not done accurately, the test lacks validity.

Take into consideration that the non-dominant hand usually scores about 10 per cent lower than the dominant hand. It is important for the validity of the test to use the same hand or an average score of both.

One repetition maximum test (1RM)

This test measures the maximum strength of chest muscle groups and is based on the maximum weight that can be moved a distance for one repetition (one rep max). The bench press for one rep max can be carried out as a test for upper body strength.

The participant should warm up with about ten reps of a light weight, followed by a minute's rest. They should then perform two warm-up sets of 2–5 reps with slightly heavier weights, with a two-minute rest between sets. Following a two-minute rest, the test is performed by doing the 1RM attempt with correct bench press technique.

▲ Figure 2.1.7 A 1RM test is often carried out using the bench press technique

If the lift is successful, there should follow a rest for another two minutes. The load is then increased by 10 per cent and the subject then attempts another lift. If there is a failed attempt to perform the lift using the correct technique, the subject should rest for two minutes and then try again with a weight about 5 per cent lower. The weights should either increase or decrease until a maximum lift is performed. The starting weight is important because the maximum weight should be lifted within five attempts.

Good 1RM scores are mostly agreed to be:

- Males 1.25 × body weight
- Females 0.8 × body weight

▼ Table 2.1.11 Rep max bench press table (weight lifted per body weight) for adults

Rating	Score (per body weight)
Excellent	>1.60
Good	1.30–1.60
Average	1.15–1.29
Below average	1.00–1.14
Poor	0.91–0.99
Very poor	<0.90

For those with less experience of lifting weights results can be variable due to technique rather than strength. Those performing this test must be taught the correct technique; otherwise it can be very dangerous. Variations in technique may also affect the score, as could the level of motivation, so it is best for the subject to motivate themselves.

The muscle energy systems also vary when reps are changed, which again will affect the score. Therefore the test may become invalid.

The equipment required is found in most gyms and health clubs. The test is simple to perform and does not require a great deal of technical expertise. The squat is considered the most convenient leg strength test in predicting sprinting and jumping ability.

Good 1RM scores are mostly agreed to be:

- males to squat carrying twice their body weight
- females to squat carrying one and half times their body weight.

For hamstrings and quadriceps strength:

- Record the one repetition maximum (1RM) for the leg curl and the same for the leg extension exercise.
- Divide the leg curl score by the leg curl extension to find the ratio for each leg.
- For each leg the curl score should be at least 80 per cent of the extension score and at least 75 per cent to reduce the chance of injury.

Power

Power is an important component of fitness that is used in many dynamic sports activities. In basketball the legs must be powerful to enable the player to jump for rebounds; a gymnast needs power for vaulting; and a rugby player needs to use power to run through a tackle.

Power is often referred to as fast strength.

Examples of activities where power is particularly important:

- Triple jump in athletics
- Games activities such as rugby
- Sprinting
- Throwing events in athletics

Key term

Power This is a combination of strength and speed.

▲ Figure 2.1.8 Strength and power are very important to the javelin thrower

Suitable test for power

Vertical jump test

Power can be assessed by using the vertical jump test, often called the sargent jump test. There are commercial jump test boards that can be fixed to the wall, which makes standardised measurement easier. The subject jumps vertically, using both feet, and then touches the calibrated scale on the board with one hand. The position of the touch is noted. The test is completed three times and the maximum height attained is recorded. If there is no test board, the subject stands next to a wall (side on) and stretches up with the hand closest to the wall. With the feet still flat on the ground, the point of the fingertips on the wall is marked with chalk. The subject then stands slightly away from the wall, jumps vertically as high as possible and touches the wall at the highest point of the jump. The difference in distance between the static reach height and the jump height becomes the score. The best of three attempts is recorded.

▼ Table 2.1.12 Norms for 16–19 year olds for vertical jump test

Gender	Excellent	Above average	Average	Below average	Poor
Male	>65 cm	50–65 cm	40–49 cm	30–39 cm	<30 cm
Female	>58 cm	47–58 cm	36–46 cm	26–35 cm	<26 cm

Standing jump test

This test measures the explosive strength of the leg muscles. The subject stands behind a line marked on the ground, with feet slightly apart. A two-foot take-off and landing is used, with swinging of the arms and bending of the knees to drive forward. The subject attempts to jump up and forward as far as possible, landing on both feet. The jump is measured from the take-off line to the nearest point of contact on the landing. The longest distance jumped is recorded after three attempts.

This is a simple test that does not take long to carry out. The technique of the jump can obscure the results, making the test invalid, unless the test and re-test technique are identical.

The norms in Table 2.1.13 are approximate for adults.

▼ Table 2.1.13 Norms for standing jump test (adults)

Rating	Males (cm)	Females (cm)
Excellent	>250	>200
Very good	241–250	191–200
Above average	231–240	181–190
Average	221–230	171–180
Below average	211–220	161–170
Poor	191–210	141–160
Very poor	<191	<141

Flexibility

This is the amount or range of movement that you can have around a joint. The structure of the joint restricts movement as well as the muscles, tendons and ligaments. As part of a healthy lifestyle or to perform sports safely and effectively, it is important to have flexibility or suppleness to prevent strains and it enables us to move quicker. If we are flexible then when we exercise we are less likely to be injured and as we go about our daily routines we can reach for objects more effectively. It also prevents stresses and strains to our muscles and joints.

▲ Figure 2.1.9 It is important to have flexibility or suppleness to prevent strains and to move quicker and more effectively

When we are flexible:
- our ligaments and supporting tissues can stretch further
- the blood flow to our muscles is improved and this helps with flexibility
- the rise in muscle temperature can help the muscle to be more flexible
- the body is used to stretching and the more able it is to stretch further.

Examples of activities where flexibility is particularly important:
- Gymnastics
- Dance
- Games activities such as hockey and football
- Table tennis
- Tennis

Ballistic stretching uses the momentum (a tendency for the body to keep moving) of a moving body or a limb in an attempt to force it beyond its normal range of motion. This is different from dynamic stretching, which involves controlled gradual stretching up to but not beyond the normal range of movement.

Suitable test for flexibility

The sit and reach test

The objective of this test is to measure the athlete's lower back and hamstring flexibility. The subject sits on the floor with legs outstretched in a straight position. They reach as far forward as possible but keeping the legs straight and in contact with the floor. The distance that the ends of the fingers are from the feet (pointing upwards) is measured. Using a 'sit and reach' box ensures more accurate measurements.

Once again this test can provide measurements that can be used in assessing any future training and also for the subject to compare performance with national norms.

Table 2.1.14 shows the national norms for 16–19 year olds.

▼ Table 2.1.14 National norms for sit and reach test for 16–19 year olds

Gender	Excellent	Above average	Average	Below average	Poor
Male	>14	11–14	7–10	4–6	<4
Female	>15	12–15	7–11	4–6	<4

The validity or accuracy of the test depends on how strictly the test is conducted and the individual's level of motivation. There are published tables to relate results to potential level of fitness and the correlation is high. This test measures the flexibility of the lower back and hamstrings only and is a valid measure of this. The reliability depends on the amount of warm-up allowed and whether the same procedures are followed each time.

The test is simple and quick to administer and perform, but the variations in arm and leg length can obscure the results.

Most norms are based on no previous warm-up, though the best results will be achieved after a warm-up or if the test is preceded by a test such as the endurance test. There is therefore a need for a consistent method of administrating the test.

IN THE NEWS

Top experts in bones and joints have advised that public health policies should focus more on the whole human frame, and not just hearts and lungs. Strategies to cut obesity by increasing physical activity, and to reduce falls in older people, have been planned by government ministers. However, leading rheumatologist experts have suggested that government strategies have failed to consider the need for flexibility and agility.

Agility

Agility is how quickly you can change direction under control and maintaining speed, balance and power, for example a netball centre changing direction quickly to receive a pass or a gymnast changing direction in a floor routine.

There are three main components of agility:

- Core strength – this will allow the performer in sport to transfer power from the feet and legs to the upper body and transfer that energy from the upper body back down to the lower body. This will help make changes of direction go more smoothly.
- Balance – the sports performer must be in control of their body at all times in order to make the right moves for their sport.
- Flexibility – the sports performer will move their body in an efficient manner through the required range of motion. Flexibility training directly improves the flow of movement by loosening up tight muscles and developing the range of movement in the joints.

▲ Figure 2.1.10 Agility is an important skill-related fitness component in netball

Examples of activities where flexibility is particularly important:

Examples of activities where flexibility is particularly important:

- Trampolining and gymnastics
- Netball and rugby
- Volleyball
- Basketball

Suitable test for agility

The Illinois agility test

The purpose of this is to test running agility.

You need a non-slip surface, a stopwatch, measuring tape and marking cones. The length of the course is 10 metres and the width (distance between the start and finish points) is 5 metres. Four cones are used to mark the start, the finish and the two turning points. Another four cones are placed down the centre, spaced 3.3 metres apart.

Subjects for the test should lie on their front (head to the start line) and hands by their shoulders. On the 'Go' command the stopwatch is started and the athlete gets up as quickly as possible and runs around the course in the direction indicated, without knocking the cones over, to the finish line, at which the timing is stopped. An excellent score is approximately under 15.2 seconds for a male and approximately less than 17 seconds for a female.

This is a simple test to administer, requiring little equipment. It establishes the players' ability to turn in different directions and at different angles. The choice of footwear and surface of the running area can affect times greatly, so these should be consistent when re-testing.

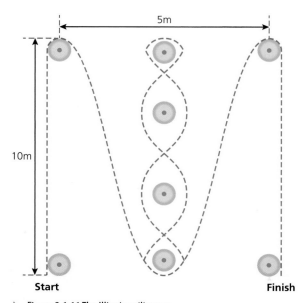

▲ Figure 2.1.11 The Illinois agility test

- Make a table with all the fitness components down one side. Choose three different sporting activities and label these at the top of the table. Now tick which components are the most important with each activity. Then present your findings.
- Using the table you have constructed, explain these physical fitness- and skill-related fitness components to a novice performer for each of your chosen activities.
- Write a report comparing and contrasting six physical fitness- and skill-related fitness requirements for all three of your activities.

Balance

This is the ability to keep your body mass or centre of mass over a base of support, e.g. a gymnast performing a handstand on a balance beam. Balance can be static (still) or dynamic (moving but in control).

Balance is a crucial component of fitness for many different activities. It can help co-ordination and fluency in movement as well as protecting the body and keeping the athlete safe in physical activities.

Examples of activities where balance is particularly important:

- Gymnastics
- Games player such as in netball, rugby and hockey
- Athletics activities such as the pole vault
- Dance activities

Suitable test for balance

Stork stand test

Before the test you warm up for approximately ten minutes. Stand upright with legs about shoulder width apart and with your hands on your hips. Lift the right leg and place the sole of the right foot against the side of the left knee. The timer shouts 'Start' and you raise the heel of your left foot to stand on your toes.

You should try to hold the balanced position for as long as possible.

The timer is stopped when the left heel touches the ground or the right foot loses contact with the knee. The time is then recorded and you rest for three minutes. Then the test is repeated but this time the left leg is lifted instead of the right. The same procedure is followed but with opposing legs. Table 2.1.15 shows norms for 16–19 year olds.

▼ Table 2.1.15 Norms for stork stand test for 16–19 year olds

Rating	Males	Females
Excellent	>50 secs	>30 secs
Above average	41–50	23–30
Average	31–40	16–22
Below average	20–30	10–15
Poor	<20	<10

Co-ordination

Another important component of fitness is **co-ordination**, which is used widely in many different physical activities and sport. We often associate good co-ordination with the ability to move different limbs at different times or to do more than one task at a time effectively, for example running and then passing a ball in rugby. A sports performer who makes a decision and then puts it into action effectively is showing good co-ordination.

Examples of activities where co-ordination is particularly important:

- Dance
- Tennis and other racket sports
- Gymnastics
- Team games such as football and netball
- Martial arts such as karate

Suitable test for co-ordination

Wall throw test

This is often referred to as the 'alternate hand wall toss test'. A mark or line is placed on the floor 2 metres from the wall. You then stand behind the line and face the wall. You throw a tennis ball against the wall with one hand in an underarm action and you attempt to catch it with the opposite hand. The ball is then thrown back against the wall and caught with the initial hand. The test continues for 30 seconds and the number of completed catches is recorded.

Table 2.1.16 shows the norms for 16–19 year olds.

▼ Table 2.1.16 Norms for wall throw test for 16–19 year olds

Rating	Score (in 30 seconds)
Excellent	>35
Good	30–35
Average	20–29
Fair	15–19
Poor	<15

Reaction time

The ability to react quickly in sports situations is crucial if you are to outwit your opponent or out-sprint another athlete.

Key term

Co-ordination This is the ability of repeating a pattern or sequence of movements with fluency and accuracy.

Key term

Reaction time This is the time it takes for you to initiate an action or movement, or the time it takes someone to make a decision to move, for example how quickly a sprinter reacts to the gun and decides to drive off the blocks.

▲ Figure 2.1.12 Good reaction time is important for a sprinter to get a good start

❓ Extend your knowledge

Reaction time is the time between the onset of the stimulus and the initiation of the response (hearing the gun in a sprint race and making the decision to drive off the blocks).
Movement time is the time it takes to move (driving from the blocks to finishing the race).
Response time is the time between the onset of the stimulus to the completion of the movement (from hearing the gun to finishing the race).

Examples of activities where reaction time is particularly important:

- Sprint start in athletics
- Receiving a serve in tennis or squash
- Team games such as basketball and hockey

Suitable test for reaction time

Ruler drop test

This is an activity, done in pairs, to show individual differences in the speed of reactions. Each pair of subjects should use a metre rule. One student, playing the role of the 'tester', places the rule vertically against the wall so that the 100 cm mark is in line with a mark on the wall just above their eye level and holds the rule against the wall with their thumb at the 95 cm mark. The second subject must stand in front of the rule and place a hand flat against the wall with their thumb over (but not touching) the 5 cm mark and focus on the 15 cm mark of the rule.

The tester then lets the rule fall and the subject must try to trap the rule by pressing their thumb on it. The point at which the thumb presses is marked and the distance the rule has dropped is measured.

Table 2.1.18 enables you to convert distance on the ruler to reaction time. For example, if you catch the ruler at the 30.5 cm mark, your reaction time is 0.25 seconds.

▼ Table 2.1.18

Distance on the ruler (centimetres)	Reaction time (seconds)
5	0.10
10	0.14
15	0.17
20	0.20
25.5	0.23
30.5	0.25
43	0.30
61	0.35
79	0.40
99	0.45

STUDY HINT

For all the components of fitness, the examiner may ask you to use data relating to all the above components. So be prepared for some simple calculations, e.g. percentage increase (shown in the practice question on page 64), and be aware of the main norms for each test result.

SUMMARY

- Cardiovascular endurance is the ability to exercise continuously without tiring.
- Tests for cardiovascular endurance include the Cooper 12-minute run/walk test and the multistage fitness test.
- Muscular endurance is the ability of the muscle or group of muscles in the body to repeatedly contract or keep going without rest. The tests for muscular endurance are the press-up test and the sit-up test.
- Speed is the maximum rate that a person can move over a specific distance or the speed of specific body parts. Tests for speed include the 30 metre sprint test.
- Strength is the ability of a muscle to exert force for a short period of time. Tests for strength include the grip strength dynamometer test and the 1RM test.
- A test for power is the vertical jump test.
- Flexibility is the amount or range of movement that you can have around a joint. A test for flexibility is the sit and reach test.
- Agility is how quickly you can change direction under control and maintaining speed, balance and power. A test for agility is the Illinois agility test.
- A test for balance is the stork stand test.
- A test for co-ordination is the alternate wall toss test.
- A test for reaction time is the ruler drop test.

Practice questions

1. Cardiovascular endurance is a component of fitness. Which of the following most accurately describes cardiovascular endurance? **(1 mark)**
   a. The ability of our heart and lungs to cope with exercise over a long period of time.
   b. The ability to use muscles over a long period of time without them getting tired.
   c. The amount of force a muscle can exert against a resistance over a long period of time.
   d. The ability to change the body's movement quickly over a long period of time.

2. What is meant by the following terms? **(3 marks)**
   - Muscular endurance
   - Flexibility
   - Agility

3. Describe **two** fitness tests for strength. **(4 marks)**

4. The following data is taken from a 20-year-old male taking the Cooper's 12-minute run/walk test:
   September 2015 – ran 2,400 metres
   December 2015 – ran 2,500 metres
   a. Calculate the percentage increase in his score. **(2 marks)**
   b. In which main component of fitness is he showing improvement? **(1 mark)**
   c. Describe another test for this component of fitness. **(3 marks)**

Chapter 2.2
Applying the principles of training

Understanding the Specification

In studying this section you should get to know the following definitions of principles of training and be able to apply them to personal exercise and training programmes:

- specificity
- overload
- progression
- reversibility.

You should also know the definition of the elements of FITT (frequency, intensity, time, type) and be able to apply these elements to personal exercise and training programmes.

You should know the different types of training and understand the key components and benefits of a warm-up and cool-down and be able to apply examples.

Principles of training

For training to be effective and to ensure that the person training gets the most out of demanding exercise sessions there needs to be a set of guidelines or rules to follow. The main principles for you to understand are specificity, overload, progression and reversibility.

1. Specificity

This principle indicates that the training undertaken should be specific and relevant to the activity or the type of sport. For instance, a sprinter would carry out more anaerobic training because the event is mostly anaerobic in nature. It is not just energy systems that have to be specific – muscle groups and actions involved in the training also have to be as specific as possible. There is, however, a consensus that a good general fitness is required before any high degree of specificity can be applied.

2. Overload

This principle underpins the need to work the body harder than normal so that there is some stress and discomfort. Adaptation and progress will follow overload because the body will respond by adapting to the stress. For instance, in weight training the lifter will eventually attempt heavier weights or an increase in repetitions, thus overloading the body. Overload can be achieved by increasing the frequency, the intensity and the duration of the activity.

3. Progression

Not only has overload got to occur, it should become progressively more difficult. Once adaptations have occurred, the performer should make even more demands on the body. It is important that progression does not mean 'overdoing it'. Training must be sensibly progressive and realistic if it

Extend your knowledge

Variance

This (extra) principle states that there should be variety in training methods. If training is too predictable, performers can become demotivated and bored. Over-use injuries are also common when training is too repetitive with one muscle group or part of the body, therefore variance can also help prevent injury.

Activity

Write a plan to outline a six-week programme and justify your activities by referring to all the principles of training listed above.

Plan an hour of exercise and include the principles of overload and specificity.

STUDY HINT

The specification demands that you know what FITT stands for and that you can give a practical example for each element. You should be able to apply examples to constructing a personal exercise and training programme.

is to be effective, otherwise injury may occur and there will be regression instead of progression.

4. Reversibility

This principle states that performance can deteriorate if training stops or decreases in intensity for any length of time. If training is stopped, then the fitness gained will be largely lost. For instance, VO_2 max and muscle strength can decrease.

Optimising training

To be able to maximise or to get the very best out of each training session or programme of sessions, a further principle should be considered. We call this the FITT principle – frequency, intensity, time and type.

The FITT principle

The FITT method ensures that athletes adhere to the principles of training. FITT stands for:

- F = frequency of training (number of training sessions each week). This will depend on the performer's level of ability and fitness. The elite athlete will train every day, whereas the lower-level club player may train only once per week. The type of training also dictates the frequency – aerobic training can be followed five or six times per week. With strength training, however, you may train only three or four times per week.
  How frequently you exercise or train depends on your ability and fitness level. You should also bear in mind the progression and overload principles. Too much training can be as harmful as not enough.
- I = intensity of the exercise undertaken. This will again take into account the individual differences of the performer and the type of training being undertaken. A 'training zone' is often created for aerobic training where heart rate ranges dictate the intensity of training. It is suggested that there should be a training intensity of 60–75 per cent of maximal heart rate reserve for the average athlete.
- T = time or duration that the training takes up. If aerobic training is required, this should be a minimum of 20 minutes or so. The duration of the training must take into account the intensity of training to be effective.
- T = type of training to be considered that fulfils specific needs. The methods of training are described earlier in this chapter and the type of sport or your role in that sport will dictate what type of training you follow. A triathlete, for example, will train all areas of fitness but pay particular attention to aerobic and muscular endurance because of the nature of the sport. For archery the type of training might include aspects of muscular endurance to keep muscles steady for effective aiming.

Example of applying training principles

The programme on page 67 illustrates two days of a week's training programme for a Premiership football player, illustrating the FITT principle:

- Frequency = (how often?), e.g. twice a week.
- Intensity = (how hard?), e.g. ten sprints.
- Time = (how long?), e.g. ten minutes' 'keep up' football skills.
- Type = (what type?), e.g. stretching.

Monday
- Rehab work such as massage and physiotherapy.
- 30 minutes – own programme of core exercises and warm-up.
- 10 minutes – run at moderate pace followed by **ballistic stretching**.
- 20 minutes – interval work with 'ladder' training for quick footwork. Ten sprints followed by stretching.
- 10 minutes – 'keep ball' in small grids.
- 10 minutes – further grid work including 4 v 1 and 3 v 2.
- 20 minutes – defenders and attackers separate drills, e.g. forwards shooting drills.
- 30 minutes – all involved in link-up play.
- 10 minutes – warm-down and further rehab where necessary.

Tuesday
- Rehab work and physiotherapy where required.
- 30 minutes – own programme of core exercises and warm-up, including ballistic stretching and ending in short sprints.
- 30 minutes – 'keep ball' and 2 teams 9 v 9 possession game with restrictions to improve quick passing and control.
- 30 minutes – grid work from 1 v 1 through to 4 v 4.
- 10 minutes – five a side with two touch restrictions.
- 20 minutes – short run intervals with 100 per cent intensity.
- 20 minutes – circuit training.
- 10 minutes – warm-down.
- 1 hour's rest.
- 10 minutes – warm-up.
- 60 minutes – weight training for strength and power.
- 10 minutes – warm-down and further rehab if necessary.

> **Key term**
>
> **Ballistic stretching** This uses the momentum (a tendency for the body to keep moving) of a moving body or a limb in an attempt to force it beyond its normal range of motion. This is different from dynamic stretching, which involves controlled gradual stretching up to but not beyond the normal range of movement.

Types of training

Training or exercise routines have a purpose, for example to improve cardiovascular endurance or flexibility. The type of training you choose can work on one or a number of components of fitness depending on your needs.

Continuous training

Continuous training activities seek to maintain and improve cardiovascular endurance. Running, cycling or swimming can be very beneficial for cardiovascular endurance. Cardiovascular adaptations can arise from continuous training, for example the heart will get bigger and stronger and the heart will not have to work so hard because each beat will force more blood around the body, therefore achieving an increase in stroke volume.

This training is related to rhythmic exercise that stresses the aerobic system. This should be carried out at a steady rate or with low intensity – between 20–30 minutes and 2 hours. This type of training ensures that there is not the build-up of lactate associated with anaerobic training.

▲ Figure 2.2.1 Aerobic capacity can be improved through continuous training

Fartlek

Fartlek is also known as 'speed play' and is often used to maintain and improve aerobic endurance. Throughout the exercise, the speed and intensity of the training are varied. In a one-hour session, for instance, there may be walking activity (which is low in intensity) and fast sprinting (which is high in intensity). This training is good for aerobic fitness because it is an endurance activity. It is good for anaerobic fitness because of the speed activities over a short period of time.

Cross-country running with sprint activities every now and again is a simplistic but reasonable way of describing fartlek; it could also be incorporated into road running. Fartlek has the added benefit of a more varied and enjoyable way of endurance training. It helps to train both the aerobic and the anaerobic energy systems and is ideal for many team sports that include intermittent sprinting and long periods of moderate activity.

Fartlek sessions need to achieve two main aims:

- to give a session that benefits the athlete's development
- to provide an environment that is varied and a worthwhile training session that encourages a high degree of effort.

❓ Extend your knowledge

Runners are known to do block fartlek sessions where they run 45–60 minutes with varying speeds. The recoveries are determined during the running. Rolling hill courses are popular routes for such sessions. These sessions are also useful when weather or availability does not permit running on a track.

✔ Check your knowledge

1. Why do fartlek rather than track running?
2. Which component/s of fitness can be improved via fartlek training?
3. What do you need to vary such training sessions?

Interval training

Interval training is one of the most popular types of training for aerobic endurance. It is adaptable to individual needs and sports. Interval training can, however, improve both aerobic and anaerobic fitness. It is called interval training because there are intervals of work and intervals of rest. For training the aerobic system, there should be intervals of slower work, which is suitable for sports such as athletics and swimming and for team games such as hockey and football.

For training the anaerobic system, there should be shorter intervals of more intense training.

The following factors should be taken into account before the design of a training session:

- **Duration** of the work interval. The work interval should be 3–10 seconds at high intensity for anaerobic and 7–8 minutes for aerobic exercise.
- **Speed** (intensity) of the work interval. This should be high (90–100 per cent of maximum intensity) for anaerobic and moderate (70–80 per cent of your maximum heart rate) for aerobic exercise.
- **Number of repetitions**. This depends on the length of the work period (the length of the training session). If the work period is short, then up to 50 repetitions is appropriate for anaerobic. For aerobic with a long work period, 3–4 repetitions are more appropriate.
- **Number of sets** of repetitions. Repetitions can be divided into sets. For example, 50 repetitions could be divided into sets of 5.
- **Duration of the rest interval**. The rest period is the length of time that the heart rate falls to about 150 bpm. Aerobic training will require a shorter rest interval for effective training.
- **Type** of activity during the rest interval. If the energy system is aerobic, then only light stretching is needed. For anaerobic activity, some light jogging may help to disperse lactic acid.

> **STUDY HINT**
>
> For examination purposes, you'll need to be able to name the following types of training:
> - ✔ continuous
> - ✔ fartlek
> - ✔ interval (including circuit, weight training plyometrics and HIIT (high-intensity interval training)).
>
> Make sure you can describe each of these types and which components of fitness they seek to improve.

Circuit training

This involves a series of exercises arranged in a particular way called a circuit because the training involves repetition of each activity. The resistance that is used in circuits relates mainly to body weight and each exercise in the circuit is designed to work on a particular muscle group. For effective training, different muscle groups should be worked at each station, with no two consecutive stations working the same muscle groups. For instance, an activity that uses the main muscle groups in the arms should be followed by an exercise involving the muscle groups in the legs. The types of exercises that are involved in circuit training are press-ups, star jumps, dips and squat thrusts.

Circuit training can also incorporate skills in the activities. A circuit for footballers, for instance, may include dribbling activities, throw-ins, shuttle runs and shooting activities.

The duration and intensity depend on the types of activities incorporated. An example would be a circuit with one minute's worth of activity, followed by one minute's worth of rest. The whole circuit could then be repeated three times. The score at the end of the circuit may be related to time or

Activity

Describe the circuit training method by drawing out a proposed circuit designed to improve muscular endurance. Present your findings.

Write a thorough explanation (two or three paragraphs) of how the circuit training method can improve muscular endurance.

❓ Extend your knowledge

Weight training is potentially dangerous – never train alone and ensure that you train within your capabilities, and do not forget to regularly re-hydrate. Poor technique can do lasting damage – weights that are too heavy for you may cause you to use poor technique; better to go lighter and perform each lift correctly.

repetitions and is a good way of motivating in training. It is also easy to see progression in fitness as more repetitions can be attempted or times improved as the weeks go by.

Typical circuit exercises:

- Running, skipping, bounding, step-ups.
- Press-ups, tricep dips, burpees or squat thrusts, chin-ups.
- Crunchies, trunk twists, dorsal raises.
- Squats, standing jumps, leg raises, sprints.

Weight training

In circuit training it is the body weight that is used as resistance to enable the body to work hard and to physiologically adapt to the training stresses. For strength to be developed, more resistance can be used – in the form of weights or against other types of resistance, such as the use of pulleys. Weight training involves a number of repetitions and sets, depending on the type of strength that needs to be developed. For throwing events in athletics, for example, training methods must involve very high resistance and low repetition. For strength endurance needed in swimming or cycling, more repetitions need to be involved, with lighter weights.

If maximum strength is required as a result of training (e.g. for athletic throwing events), include a high resistance activity (high percentage of your maximum), with low number of repetitions (number of times you repeat the movement), e.g. 80 per cent maximum strength with three sets of five repetitions. If strength endurance is required then higher reps and lower resistance is best – 3 sets of 20 reps at 55 per cent max strength.

Plyometrics

Plyometrics is a form of training exercise that involves rapid and repeated stretching and contracting of the muscles, designed to increase strength and power. This type of training is specifically intended to improve dynamic strength. Plyometrics improves the speed with which muscles contract and therefore affects power.

If muscles have previously been stretched, they tend to generate more force when contracted. Any sport that involves sprinting, throwing and jumping will benefit from this type of training, as will players of many team sports such as netball or rugby.

Plyometrics involves bounding, hopping and jumping, when muscles have to work concentrically (jumping up) and eccentrically (landing).

One type of jumping used in this training method is called in-depth jumping, which is when the athlete jumps on to and off boxes. This type of training is strenuous on the muscles and joints and the athlete must be reasonably fit before attempting it. As usual, it is important that the muscles are warmed and stretched before beginning. Footballers often do plyometrics for increasing the power in their legs.

IN THE NEWS

The British tennis player Andy Murray has been seen preparing for his Wimbledon matches with a modified press-up activity – this is an example of plyometrics. Some call it the 'donkey-kick' press-up, which is an explosive-type movement, much more intense and dynamic than a normal press-up. You do the kick when you're down, then push up as your legs are coming back down to the ground.

The pectorals, triceps and core muscles are worked hard in this activity, which involves shortening and lengthening the muscles at speed to generate power and create more force.

▲ Figure 2.2.2 Andy Murray uses plyometrics to prepare for his tennis matches

High-intensity interval training (HIIT)

High-intensity interval training is a cardiorespiratory training technique that alternates brief speed and recovery intervals to increase the overall intensity of a workout.

Most endurance workouts, such as walking, running or stair climbing, are performed at a moderate intensity, or an exertion level of 5–6 on a scale of 0–10. High-intensity intervals are done at an exertion level of 7 or higher and are typically sustained for between 30 seconds and 3 minutes, although they can be as short as 8–10 seconds or as long as 5 minutes – the higher the intensity, the shorter the speed interval. Recovery intervals are equal to or longer than the speed intervals.

HIIT training not only helps performance, it also improves the ability of the muscles to burn fat. A typical HIIT training session usually lasts about 20–30 minutes.

❓ Extend your knowledge

Some typical HIIT sessions:

- **On a track**. Warm up with five laps at an easy pace. Gradually speed up so that you end up running briskly. Then do 200 metres at maximal sprint effort followed by 400 metres gentle jog. Repeat six times.

- **On a treadmill**. Set the incline to 1 per cent. Warm up by running gently, gradually building speed, for 10 minutes. On an effort scale of 1–10, you should be at 5–6 by the end. Run 30 seconds at close to maximal speed; jog gently for 3 minutes. Repeat 4–6 times.

- **On a bike**. Following a short warm-up, try 4–6 bouts of maximal sprint efforts, each lasting for 30 seconds, and follow with 4 minutes of easy spinning recovery.

▲ Figure 2.2.3 HIIT is a cardiorespiratory training technique that alternates brief speed and recovery intervals to increase the overall intensity of a workout

IN THE NEWS

A seven-minute workout app based on research has recently been developed, showing the benefit of HIIT. It has been found that 20 minutes of an intense workout burns an average of 15 calories per minute – twice the amount used on a long run.

Other HIIT-type training activities typically involve 60 seconds of exercise near your maximum effort, followed by a recovery period of the same amount, repeated for 20 minutes, three times a week. Your peak effort is around 80–90 per cent of your maximum heart rate.

You can do HIIT on a bike, running, swimming, on gym equipment like a cross trainer, or by sprinting up and down the stairs.

The warm-up

The key components of a warm-up are as follows.

1. **Pulse raising**. This includes exercises that slowly increase heart rate and gradually increase body temperature, for example jogging, cycling, skipping or gentle running.

2. **Mobility**. Exercises that take the joints through their full range of movement (ROM), for example arm swings, hip circles, high-knees activities.

3. **Stretching**. This can include developmental stretches, gradually increasing the difficulty of each stretch or dynamic stretches that include more ballistic movements (for example, lunges) or static stretches where the body remains still or static while stretching. Examples of stretches include open and close the gate, groin walk for more dynamic exercises and slowly trying to touch your toes for more static stretches.

4. **Dynamic movements**. This involves movements that show a change of speed and direction, for example shuttle runs.
5. **Skill rehearsal**. This involves practising or rehearsing common movement patterns and skills that will be used in the activity, for example dribbling drills for football or passing drills for netball.

▲ Figure 2.2.4 Whatever the level of the sport, whether it is serious competition or recreational play, you should be prepared for the activity by carrying out an effective warm-up

Physical benefits of a warm-up

The warm-up enables the body to prepare for exercise and decreases the likelihood of injury and muscle soreness. There is also a release of adrenaline that will start the process of speeding up the delivery of oxygen to the working muscles. An increase in muscle temperature will help to ensure that there is a ready supply of energy and that the muscle becomes more flexible to prevent injury.

It is crucial that all performers in physical activities and sport take appropriate steps to prepare for vigorous activity through an effective warm-up and, following the activity, a cool-down. This applies to all physical activities at all levels. If you are a beginner it is just as important to warm up properly.

❓ Extend your knowledge

Factors to be taken into consideration before planning a warm-up/cool-down:

- Size of group – large/small
- Age of participants – young/old
- Sex of participants – gender/whether group is mixed sex
- Experience of participants – novice or expert/skill level
- Individual fitness levels – trained/unfit/previous injury/flexibility/size/weight
- Medical conditions – asthma/diabetes/other named conditions
- Disability

❓ Extend your knowledge

Warm-up for professional golf

Stretch your arms by raising them above your head with your palms together. Stretch your fingertips on your left hand higher than the ones on your right hand and then vice versa. Hit up to 50 practice shots to loosen up before the first tee. Use smooth, slow swings to loosen up.

STUDY HINT

It may be helpful to learn a summary of the benefits of a warm-up:
- ✔ Gradually raises body temperature and heart rate
- ✔ Improves flexibility/pliability of muscle fibres
- ✔ Increases pliability of ligaments and tendons
- ✔ Increases the blood flow and the amount of oxygen to the muscles
- ✔ Increases the speed of muscle contractions

It's also helpful if you can construct a warm-up using pulse raiser, mobility, stretching, dynamic movements and skill rehearsal.

▲ Figure 2.2.5 The warm-up and the cool-down are important elements of a fitness training programme

The cool-down

The key components of a cool-down are:

1. Low-intensity exercises – gradually lower the pulse rate and the heart rate and reduce the body's temperature, for example easy movement exercises or light running/jogging.
2. Stretching – includes steady and static stretches, for example hamstring stretch.

Physical benefits of a cool-down

The cool-down is important for effective training. If light exercise follows training, then the oxygen can more effectively be flushed through the muscle tissue and will oxidise any lactic acid, which needs to be dispersed. Cool-downs also prevent blood pooling in the veins, which can cause dizziness.

The cool-down is crucial in:

- helping the body's transition back to a resting state
- gradually lowering heart rate
- gradually lowering temperature
- circulating blood and oxygen
- gradually reducing breathing (respiratory) rate
- increasing the removal of waste products such as lactic acid
- reducing the risk of muscle soreness (or delayed onset of muscle soreness – DOMS) and stiffness
- reducing the risk of blood pooling
- reducing the risk of damage to joints
- aiding recovery by stretching muscles, i.e. lengthening and strengthening muscles for next workout/use.

IN THE NEWS

Use of ice jackets

Marathon world record holder Paula Radcliffe needs to cool off. So says Nike, which has developed the 'PreCool Vest' to stop athletes boiling over while performing activities such as the marathon and the 10,000 m.

According to the publicity spiel, the jacket 'slows the rise of an athlete's body temperature by 19%, reducing the risk of overheating and heat stroke and allowing the athlete a higher level of performance'. A Nike spokesperson adds: 'It's an amazing fact but only 25% of our total body's energy goes into moving muscle while 75% is used to regulate heat.'

SUMMARY

- The four principles of training are that it should:
  - be specific to the sport
  - work the body harder than normal (overload)
  - progress incrementally
  - reversible – all training achievements are reversible if training stops or slows down.
- The FITT principle includes frequency, intensity, time and type.
- Continuous training seeks to maintain and improve cardiovascular endurance.
- Fartlek is also known as 'speed play' and is often used to maintain and improve aerobic endurance.
- Interval training is one of the most popular types of training for aerobic endurance but can improve both aerobic and anaerobic fitness.
- Circuit training involves a series of exercises arranged in a particular way called a circuit because the training involves repetition of each activity.
- Weight training involves a number of repetitions and sets, depending on the type of strength that needs to be developed.
- Plyometrics improves the speed with which muscles contract and therefore affects power.
- High-intensity interval training (HIIT) is a cardiorespiratory training technique that alternates brief speed and recovery intervals to increase the overall intensity of a workout.
- The benefits of a warm-up are that it:
  - improves flexibility
  - increases pliability of ligaments and tendons
  - increases the amount of oxygen to the muscles
  - increases the speed of muscle contractions.
- If light exercise follows training as a cool-down, then the oxygen can more effectively be flushed through the muscle tissue and will oxidise any lactic acid.

Practice questions

1. Using a weight training programme as a basis for your answer, describe the principles of training. **(10 marks)**

2. Explain why an athlete might use continuous training to improve performance. **(4 marks)**

3. Describe plyometrics as a training method and state what this type of training seeks to achieve. **(4 marks)**

4. Using a practical example, describe an effective warm-up before performing a sports activity. **(5 marks)**

5. Why is it important for a sports performer to carry out a cool-down following a competitive activity? **(4 marks)**

Understanding the Specification

You should know and understand how the risk of injury in physical activity and sport can be minimised and be able to apply examples, including:

- personal protective equipment
- correct clothing/footwear
- appropriate level of competition
- lifting and carrying equipment safely
- use of warm-up and cool-down.

You should also know the potential hazards in a range of physical activity and sport settings and be able to apply examples, including:

- sports hall
- fitness centre
- playing field
- artificial outdoor areas
- swimming pool.

Minimising the risk of injury in physical activity and sport

The following are ways of helping to prevent injuries or health problems associated with physical activities and sport.

Personal protective equipment

The risks arising from some hazards can be limited by using **personal protective equipment** (PPE), for instance when people wear protective gloves while handling cleaning equipment or a rugby player wears a gum shield. An example of a piece of protective equipment in a physical activity is a squash player wearing protective goggles to minimise the risk of impact with the ball. Other examples of personal protective equipment include:

- scrumcaps in rugby and safety helmets in canoeing
- gloves as a cricket wicketkeeper or hockey goalkeeper
- shin pads in football and hockey.

Key term

Personal protective equipment PPE (including correct clothing and footwear) is defined by the government's Health and Safety Executive as 'all equipment (including clothing affording protection against the weather) which is intended to be worn or held by a person at work and which protects him (or her) against one or more risks to his health or safety'.

▲ Figure 2.3.1 The risks arising from some hazards can be limited by using protective equipment

Correct clothing and footwear

It is also important to wear the correct clothing and footwear for the sport to be played, for example football boots with appropriate studs in football and warm, waterproof clothing for outdoor adventurous activities.

Appropriate level of competition

Make sure that you are fit for physical activity and sport. If you are going to undertake an activity requiring stamina, make sure you have good cardiorespiratory fitness. If in basketball, for example, you are required to stretch suddenly, make sure that you have worked on your flexibility to prevent injury.

Be aware of the main principles of fitness training that have been covered in this book. Any exercise and training programme must take into account the individual. The participant's age, time available, equipment available and skill level must all be taken into consideration before the principles of training are applied.

Each participant must get to a particular skill level and have good technique before performing seriously in physical activity and sport. Exercise and training should include basic skills which when practised enough become almost second nature. Injury is much less likely the higher your personal skill level. Ensure that skills and techniques follow technical models of how the skill ought to be performed to ensure personal health and safety.

Lifting and carrying equipment safely

Back strains and even broken limbs have been caused by incorrect methods of lifting and carrying sports equipment. The correct technique for lifting heavy equipment involves bending the knees rather than the back.

Some equipment needs to be lifted with mechanical assistance. If there are special instructions concerning the method of lifting or moving a particular piece of equipment these should always be followed.

Additional hazards can arise during assembly of equipment. For instance, a trampoline should be put up only by people who have been trained to do it properly, otherwise there is a danger of the trampoline's legs springing up and causing injury.

Warm-up and cool-down

Whatever the level of the physical activity or sport – whether it is serious competition or just recreational play – you should be prepared for it by carrying out an effective warm-up. A cool-down is equally important and should take place immediately after exercise. Refer to the previous chapter for further detail on the steps involved.

Always ensure that your training is safe. After warming up sufficiently your exercise regime should suit your age, ability and physical fitness. You should also ensure that you do not push yourself too hard and that you 'listen' to your body and stop if any exercise hurts or you are getting unduly tired.

IN THE NEWS

Injury statistics (Health and Safety Executive, 2015)

(The report covers a recent five-year period.)

Fatal injuries to members of the public:

'A child was crushed by an unsecured mobile goal post while playing on a football field. Children moved the posts from their usual secured storage place so that they could use them. The goal posts were very heavy and unstable, and needed secure fixing before use.'

? Extend your knowledge

Of the 999 major injuries recorded:

- 349 injuries (35 per cent) resulted from a slip or trip (106 involved sliding on a slippery surface).
- 75 involved lost footing, 62 falling over an obstruction and 60 slipping while playing sports.
- 79 injuries (8 per cent) resulted from handling, lifting or carrying a load (of which 39 involved an awkward or sharp object and 24 involved a heavy object).

Non-fatal injuries to members of the public:

- In a five-year period there were 3,675 non-fatal injuries to members of the public in the sports and recreation industry. Of these:
  - 1,430 (39 per cent) resulted from a slip or trip (762 involved slipping while playing sports).
  - 1,347 (37 per cent) resulted from a fall from a height (297 involved falling while playing sport).

Common types of sports injuries

Head injuries

A likely head injury in sport is to be knocked unconscious and to suffer from concussion. If the player has suffered light concussion then they can return to play after about 15 minutes of rest following a medical check. If, however, the player is unconscious, check their airway is clear and call a trained first aider. A hospital visit is advisable. They may need at least a week to make a full recovery after severe concussion. Post-concussion syndrome (a collection of symptoms that can last for several weeks or months after the concussion) can occur after weeks or months if proper treatment is not given after the injury.

? Extend your knowledge

Exercising safely

- Identify the individual's training goal.
- Identify medium- and long-term goals.
- Identify the fitness components to be improved.
- Establish the energy systems to be used.
- Identify the muscle groups that will be used.
- Evaluate the fitness components involved.
- Use a training diary.
- Vary the programme to maintain motivation.
- Include rest in the programme for recovery.
- Evaluate and reassess goals.

STUDY HINT

Injuries and their treatment are not directly examined in the specification, but background knowledge of injuries will help your understanding of how to reduce risks and injuries.

? Extend your knowledge

Concussion

Professional rugby players are not allowed to play for three weeks after experiencing concussion.

IN THE NEWS

The number of reported concussions in English rugby rose by 59 per cent in 2013–14 compared with the previous season, the latest annual injury audit has shown. The audit recorded 86 cases in 2013–14 after 54 the season before. Concussion in rugby was highlighted in the World Cup in 2015, when George North continued to play on for Wales against England after appearing to be knocked out. World Rugby has since said it will look into using video replays to assist medical staff in making their decisions.

▲ Figure 2.3.2 Rugby players may experience concussion after a blow to the head

Spinal injury

Any injury to the spine should be treated extremely seriously. It could result in lasting damage to someone's health and their fitness to operate normally, let alone play sport. Damage to the spinal cord may cause very painful conditions. A break in the cord high up in the spine is usually fatal. If there is a suspected injury to the spine it is important to get expert help immediately without moving the injured person. Spinal injuries can be caused by incidents such as a collapsed rugby scrum or falling off a horse in equine events.

Fractures

Bone fractures can be serious injuries. As well as damaging the bone they often injure the tissues around the bone such as tendons, ligaments, muscles and skin. A fracture occurs when there is a physical impact or indirect blow to the bone. Anyone involved in contact sports is in danger of sustaining a fractured bone.

To treat the fracture, cover and elevate the injured limb and keep it completely still. The casualty should go to hospital for treatment. The limb will probably be put in a cast to keep it still while the bone heals. The injured person can be back in training after 5–12 weeks.

Dislocations

Dislocation involves movement of a joint from its normal position and is caused by a blow or a fall. When a joint has a lot of pressure put upon it in a certain direction, the bones that usually join in the joint disconnect. The joint capsule often tears because of this movement of bones, along with the ligaments involved. The exerciser or sports person will have limited movement and will experience severe pain.

Sprain

This is a tear to a ligament and is often caused by an overstretch. Ankles, knees and wrists are particularly susceptible to sprains.

Ankle sprains, caused by going over on your ankle, are common among people involved in sport or outdoor activities. Sometimes a 'snap' or 'tear' is felt or heard. Treatment involves rest, ice, compression and elevation (RICE). Do not remove the shoe until ice has reduced the ankle swelling. Recovery takes between one week and three months, depending on the grade of injury. The usual recovery time is two weeks.

Strain

This is a twist or tear to a muscle or a tendon. Causes include over-use of the joint, force or overstretching.

Blisters

A blister is the body's way of trying to put protection between the skin and what is causing friction, e.g. in a footballer's case, their boot.

The skin is in various layers. Friction and force cause these layers to tear. Fluid called serum flows in between the damaged layers, producing a bubble of liquid. The pain begins when this swelling rubs against another surface.

To treat blisters, the first thing you have to do is cleanse the skin with a sterilising solution. Then, with a sterilised needle, puncture the blister – make sure you do not damage the skin, otherwise it could create further problems. The next step is to put a protective covering over the blister to prevent infections.

The amount of time a blister takes to heal depends upon how big it is, but on average a couple of days is enough.

Risk assessment

To be able to prepare a **risk assessment** it is important to identify the following:

- The health and safety hazards in a given situation. This includes identifying equipment faults, use of chemicals, other substances hazardous to health and the possibility of spillages.
- The purpose of the assessment. Identify the level of risk. The assessment is designed mostly to minimise injury to participants and workers. It is also designed to ensure that the activity involved can be successful with no injury or accident but hopefully keeping the pleasure and excitement. A safe environment is crucial if physical activity is to be successful.
- The risks involved. Participants, coaches, supervisors, etc. must be aware of their responsibilities in limiting the risks in any sports activity.

Key term

Risk assessment This is the technique by which you measure the chances of an accident happening, anticipate what the consequences would be and plan actions to prevent it.

STUDY HINT
Be able to identify a hazard for each area named in the specification:
- ✔ Sports hall
- ✔ Fitness centre
- ✔ Playing field
- ✔ Artificial outdoor areas
- ✔ Swimming pool

Key terms

Hazard Something that has the potential to cause harm.
Risk The chance that someone will be harmed by the hazard.

❓ Extend your knowledge

The main causes of accidents are:

- objects falling – e.g. a container falling off a shelf in a leisure centre
- trips and falls – e.g. a path leading up to a sports facility may be uneven
- electric shock – e.g. from a hi-fi used to provide music for an aerobics session
- crowds – e.g. supporters at a football match tripping over each other
- poisoning – e.g. by toxic chemicals used in a swimming pool
- being hit by something – e.g. a javelin
- fire – e.g. in the changing rooms of a sports centre
- explosion – e.g. in the store area of a leisure centre
- asphyxiation – e.g. by chemicals used for cleaning.

The risks should be calculated, specialist equipment used and record sheets and other documents kept up to date.

- Procedures for monitoring or checking that risks are kept to a minimum. If there are any changes to the planning of an activity, these should be reviewed to identify their levels of success. There may be other equipment to buy to make the environment safe or new procedures to be used. All this must be planned within an identified time cycle.

The hazard is often supervised so that the risks are minimised. A supervisory function is performed by, for example, a lifeguard at a swimming pool, spotters around a trampoline (those that stand around the trampoline to stop the performer jumping off) or a coach supporting a gymnast on the beam.

Identifying potential hazards in a range of physical activity and sport settings

The area in which the activity takes place must be looked at carefully to recognise possible **hazards**. The facilities and equipment that are used in physical activities often carry warnings of possible injuries and these must be noted.

There may be obvious **risks** associated with the activity, the equipment or the facilities – for example, on an all-weather surface, if a player falls or slides they may experience friction burns.

It is important to take care with anyone who may not be fully aware of risks, for instance children or those with learning difficulties, or someone new to a job in a leisure centre or a beginner in a sports activity. Once those who are at particular risk have been identified, an assessment of how they might be harmed needs to be made and safety procedures put into place to protect them.

There must be an assessment of how dangerous a particular hazard is and then whether the risks associated with that hazard are high, moderate or low. If the hazard is particularly dangerous and the risks are high, more care clearly needs to be taken.

Examples of hazards in a sports hall:

- Exercise/gym equipment
- Walls
- Doors
- Windows
- Lighting
- Hard floor
- Other participants

Examples of hazards in a fitness centre:

- Equipment (broken or position)
- Flooring
- Windows
- Free weights
- Other participants

Examples of hazards on a playing field:
- Litter, including broken bottles and dog excrement
- Goal posts and other semi-permanent equipment
- Movable equipment
- Fencing
- Pitch surface
- Other participants

Examples of hazards on artificial outdoor areas:
- Surface of pitch
- Litter, including broken bottles and dog excrement
- Goal posts and other semi-permanent equipment
- Movable equipment
- Fencing
- Other participants

Examples of hazards in and around a swimming pool:
- Water
- Chemicals in the water
- Surface of surrounding area
- Equipment
- Weather (if outdoors)
- Other participants

STUDY HINT

Don't get hazard and injury mixed up. If you are asked to identify a hazard, do not give the injury that might be caused by the hazard. For instance, a hazard might be a broken bottle on a playing field – the hazard is not the cut that might be caused by the broken glass.

In many cases it may be possible to remove the hazard altogether, for instance an uneven path is declared out of bounds or a broken indoor football goal is removed from a sports hall.

In some cases the hazard has to be made safer to reduce the risks – for example, glass in a door that is used frequently can be replaced with non-breakable plastic, or a trampoline can be surrounded by additional safety mats.

SUMMARY

- Risks of injury in sport can be minimised by using personal protective equipment, correct clothing/footwear, appropriate level of competition, lifting and carrying equipment safely and through the use of a warm-up and a cool-down.
- Make sure you are fit for physical activity and sport. If you are intending to be involved in an activity requiring stamina, make sure you have good cardiorespiratory fitness.
- Each participant must get to a particular skill level and have good technique before performing seriously in physical activity and sport.
- The correct technique for lifting heavy equipment involves bending the knees rather than the back.
- Hazard is something that has the potential to cause harm.
- Risk is the chance that someone will be harmed by the hazard.
- Common hazards in sport include playing surface, equipment, litter, water (swimming) and other participants.

✔ Check your understanding

1. What is meant by a hazard in physical activities?
2. What hazards are associated with the gymnasium/sports hall/ fitness centre?
3. What hazards are associated with a playing field and an artificial outdoor area?
4. What hazards are associated with a swimming pool?
5. How would you reduce the risk of hazards in each of these areas?

Practice questions

1. Which of the following is a potential hazard of a school playing field?   **(1 mark)**
   a. Correct footwear
   b. Discarded litter
   c. The sports equipment
   d. Other players

2. Describe an occasion when correct carrying technique will reduce the chance of injury during or preparing for a physical activity.   **(2 marks)**

3. Describe three ways of minimising risks when swimming in an indoor swimming pool.   **(3 marks)**

4. Identify a hazard in a fitness centre and explain how you would reduce the risks associated with that hazard.
                                                                (4 marks)

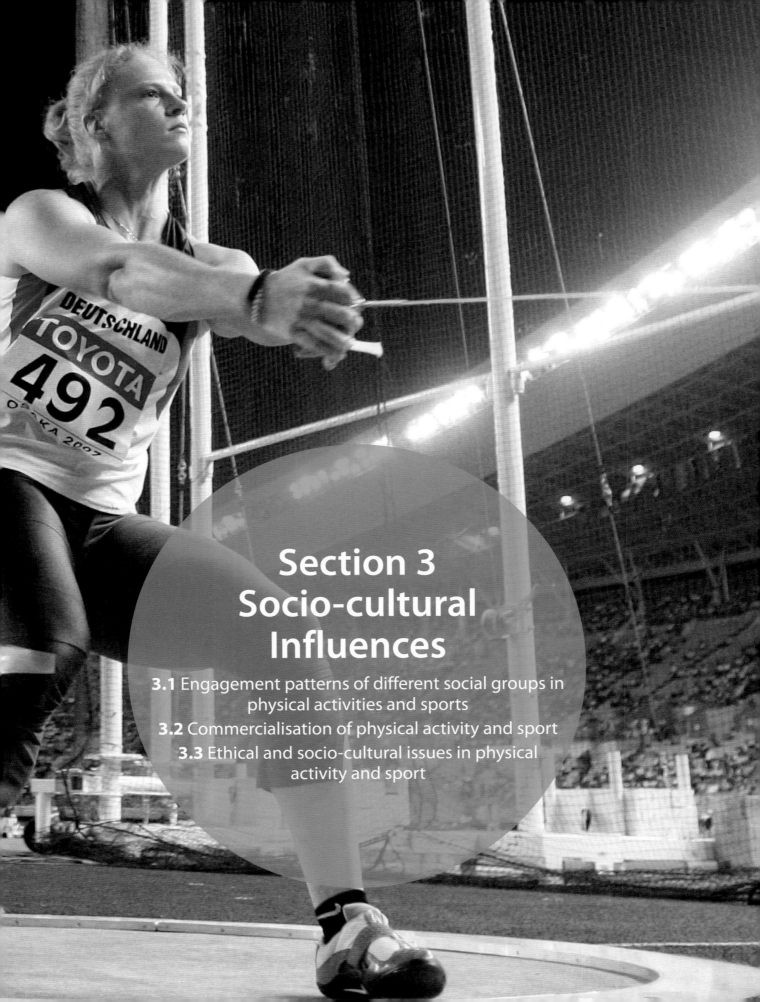

Section 3
Socio-cultural Influences

3.1 Engagement patterns of different social groups in physical activities and sports

3.2 Commercialisation of physical activity and sport

3.3 Ethical and socio-cultural issues in physical activity and sport

Chapter 3.1
Engagement patterns of different social groups in physical activities and sports

Understanding the Specification

You should be familiar with current trends in different social groups' participation in physical activity and sport.

You should understand how different socio-cultural factors can affect participation and understand strategies that can be used to improve participation through promotion, provision and access.

You should be able to apply examples from physical activity/sport to these participation issues.

Current trends in participation in physical activity and sport in the UK

For the health and fitness of British citizens, it is important to know and understand the current position regarding physical activity. The trends are related to groups in society such as males and females or those of a particular age group, for example. This information can be used to target particular groups to increase the levels of exercise and sports activities to hopefully lead to a healthier and more active population so that individuals' health and well-being can be improved.

Participation for 14 plus in activities lasting at least 30 minutes a week

This group for those who are aged 14 plus has been of particular interest because this is the age at which the trend for lifelong healthy exercise is often set.

The target for **Sport England** is to increase participation in sport for people aged 14 and older for at least 30 minutes once a week. Participation in sport for at least 30 minutes a week has remained fairly steady over the past few years, at around 33 per cent of adults.

Participation in sport 16–24 year olds

Those who participate in **sport** from the age of 16 up to 24 are again of interest because of setting lifetime habits and to improve health and well-being.

- Since 2005/6, the percentage of 16–24 year olds participating in sport has decreased (down from 76.8 per cent to 72.1 per cent).
- 54.7 per cent of 16–24 year olds participate in sport once a week for 30 minutes or more. (Source: Sport England 2015)

Key terms

Sport England This organisation tries to help communities develop sporting habits for life. It funds other organisations and projects to get people more involved in sport and to help those who wish to pursue sport to the highest level.

Sport This involves organised competition between individuals or teams that includes physical activity.

Participation 24 years plus

Those who participate over the age of 24 are likely to be fitter and healthier but are still in the minority and so are a continuing concern as an age group.

- 31.4 per cent of adults 26 years or older participate in sport once a week for 30 minutes or more.
- 40.1 per cent of men and 30.5 per cent of women in England participate in moderate intensity level sport at least once a week.

Other participation data from Sport England (2015)

- In 2011 43 per cent of 5–16 year olds' main method of getting to and from school was walking, while the main method for 33 per cent of this age group was being driven to school in a car/van. Just 2 per cent used a bike to travel to school as their main mode of transport.
- In 2011/12 80 per cent of 5–15 year olds reported that they had done some form of competitive sport in the last 12 months. More than three quarters (77 per cent) had taken part in a competitive sport in school while 37 per cent had taken part outside of school.

❓ Extend your knowledge

Participation in cycling

- One quarter of respondents in the survey indicated that they were more likely to take a UK cycling holiday as a result of the London 2012 Games.
- Immediately following the 2012 Olympic Games 52 per cent of respondents indicated that they were motivated to cycle as a result of the achievements of Team GB.
- The largest influence of the Olympics has been indicated among social riding and occasional rides for light exercise. The latter reflected an increase of almost 30 per cent in cyclists motivated to undertake the activity, while the potential for social cycling increased by 11 per cent.
- The success of mass participation programmes such as Sky Ride has continued, with 200,000 people taking part in cycling in major city events and 835 local events in 2011. 700,000 new people are now riding their bikes once a month as a result of the British Cycling and Sky partnership since 2008.
- British Cycling estimates that participation in cycling has increased by 20 per cent since the 2008 Beijing Olympic Games, with more than 200,000 people with a disability cycling at least once per week in 2015. (Source: UK Sport 2015)

❓ Extend your knowledge

Participation compared with the rest of Europe

Participation rates in the UK are above those for Europe as a whole, with 41 per cent of adult Europeans exercising or playing sport once a week compared with 48.5 per cent in England. Rates are, however, still significantly below the countries with the highest levels (70 per cent in Sweden, 68 per cent in Denmark and 66 per cent in Finland). Significant investment has not led to the large boost in participation hoped for from the London 2012 Olympic Games and indeed regular participation in sport has fallen since London 2012.

Key term

Participation rates This refers to the number of people within a group who are involved in sport compared with those who are not. For example, in a school the participation rates of girls in extra-curricular sport could be 30 per cent. In other words, three out of every ten girls in the school are members of a sports team or club.

IN THE NEWS

As reported in the media in 2015 and published by the Department of Health, young people who participate in sport every day are twice as likely to have high levels of happiness than those who participate in sport on two or fewer days a week.

Popular sports

In terms of participation the five most popular activities among adults in the UK are (figures are approximate – UK Sport 2015):

- walking (46 per cent)
- swimming (35 per cent)
- keep fit/yoga, including aerobics and dance exercise (22 per cent)
- cycling (19 per cent)
- cue sports – billiards, snooker and pool (17 per cent).

IN THE NEWS

In the year that Andy Murray won Wimbledon (2013), there was a fall in the number of people who played tennis at least once a week. Yet with a British tennis player winning such a prestigious tournament, it would have been expected that participation would rise.

Sport England's Active People Survey found that 406,000 people played in the year 2013 to October – a fall of 39,000 on the previous 12-month period.

Activity

Table 3.1.1 shows the number of people aged 16 and over playing at least 30 minutes of sport at moderate intensity at least once a week. Analyse this data and:

a. Rank order the most popular sports in April 2013.
b. Which sport's participation rates fell the most?
c. Which sport's participation rates rose the most?

▼ Table 3.1.1 Data from government UK source

	Apr 2012–Apr 2013	Apr 2011–Apr 2012	% change
Swimming	2.89 m	2.82 m	+2.39%
Athletics	1.96 m	1.99 m	−1.82%
Football	1.94 m	2.2 m	−11.76%
Cycling	1.87 m	1.93 m	-3.54%
Golf	772,800	908,000	−14.89%
Tennis	424,300	420,300	+0.95%
Squash	257,700	281,100	−8.32%
Cricket	189,400	211,300	−10.36%
Rugby union	166,400	197,500	−15.75%
Boxing	150,100	139,200	+7.83%

Participation by gender

Men are more likely than women to participate in sports activities – about 51 per cent of men compared with 36 per cent of women (UK Sport 2015). In general, participation rates decrease with age. Approximately 72 per cent of young adults (aged 16–19) compared with 54 per cent of adults aged 30–44 and 14 per cent of adults aged 70 and over participate in at least one activity (excluding walking). Overall, men are more likely than women to have participated in an organised competition, with about 40 per cent of men competing compared with 14 per cent of women.

Participation rates by age

The proportion of adults who take part in at least one sport or physical activity, with the exception of walking, generally decreases with age.

- Including walking, 77 per cent of 16–19 year olds take part in at least one physical activity compared with 30 per cent of people aged 70 and over.
- Participation rates that excluded walking range from 72 per cent of 16–19 year olds to 14 per cent of people aged 70 and over.

Walking is the most popular activity for all age groups. Participation rates in walking increase from 29 per cent of those aged 16–19 to 40 per cent of those aged 45–59, after which they decline.

Activities such as soccer, cue sports, running and cycling are generally more popular with the younger age groups and the rates of participation for each of these activities decrease with age. However, participation in golf is maintained at a fairly similar level up to age 69, with the average age of participants being about 42.

Participation rates in swimming and keep fit/yoga remain at similar levels between the ages of 16 and 44, after which they fall. Participants in bowls peak among 60–69 year olds.

Participation rates for other different social groups

Disability

Between April 2014 and March 2015 17.2 per cent of people aged 16 years and over with a long-term limiting illness or disability played sport once a week, an increase from 15 per cent in 2005/6. This can be compared with those without a disability at 39.3 per cent, showing that relatively few people with a disability are involved in sport.

Ethnicity

Between April 2014 and March 2015, 37.9 per cent of people from black and minority ethnic groups aged 16 years or over played sport once a week, 768,200 more than in 2005/6.

Of people describing themselves as white–British, 35.1 per cent aged 16 years or over played sport once a week.

Among different ethnic groups, participation varies very little for men. Among women, however, those from white backgrounds are much more likely to take part in sport compared with those from Chinese, black and other ethnic minority backgrounds, with a low of 21 per cent for females from Asian backgrounds.

Across sport as a whole:

- 89 per cent of those who take part are from white backgrounds
- 11 per cent are from non-white backgrounds (88 per cent of the English population are from white backgrounds), but this varies in specific sports
- in basketball and cricket, more than a third are from a non-white background
- badminton and football also have a higher than average proportion of players from a non-white background
- non-white players make up a comparatively small share of cyclists and golfers.

IN THE NEWS

Earnings of professional sportswomen

Although many sports have moved into the 21st century and award equal prize money for men and women in major competitions, 30 per cent of sports, including football, cricket and squash, refuse to move forward, as highlighted in 2014 by the BBC.

When Arsenal's men's and women's teams both won the FA Cup in 2014, the women were paid £5,000 as a team and the men received £1.8 million. It doesn't stop with just the performers of the sport. Disparity in wages can be found behind the scenes, with female coaches, managers and sports journalists discovering that more junior male colleagues are being paid more.

Socio-economic groups

The rate of participation among people aged 16 years and over is greater in those from higher socio-economic groups than those from lower socio-economic groups – 38.7 per cent participate in the higher socio-economic groups while 25.7 per cent participate from manual and unemployed socio-economic groups.

The main factors affecting participation in physical activity and sport

There are many influences on whether people participate in physical activity and sport. There are, of course, people who show no interest in sports whatsoever, but even those may be interested in keeping healthy and may well do some exercise or consider carefully what they eat.

❓ Extend your knowledge

Despite fewer than one in ten pupils attending fee-paying schools in the UK, more than four in ten of the British athletes who won medals at London 2012 were schooled privately. Alongside the success of state-educated athletes including Jessica Ennis, Mo Farah and Greg Rutherford and cyclist Victoria Pendleton, half the gold medal winners were educated privately, including cyclist Chris Hoy and sailor Ben Ainslie.

Age

The average life expectancy has increased and so there are more and more older people who could take advantage of sports opportunities. There are more veterans' teams in a variety of sports and there is a growing awareness that activity in old age can enrich the quality of life experiences. Sport, however, is often perceived as a 'young person's activity' and older age groups may lack confidence in participating.

IN THE NEWS

Age is a factor in participation: in 2015, about 55 per cent of 16–25 year olds took part in at least one sport session a week, compared with about 32 per cent of older adults (26 plus).

▲ Figure 3.1.1 As people reach old age, participation in sport decreases for some

Age can affect participation in sport in the UK, with many participants in school stopping sports activities in their teenage years. This could be because of other competing interests such as school work or playing computer games, or simply through a general lack of interest or that sport is not 'cool' enough and does not fit in with their own or their peers' self-image. As people get older they become less likely to participate in sport and more likely to participate in more 'keep fit' activities. Then as people reach old age again participation drops off. This may be because of poor health and perceived lack of fitness or the lack of suitable activities, accessibility or transport.

❓ Extend your knowledge

Health problems

There are genuine health reasons for some people not to participate in sport, although many medical practitioners will encourage an active lifestyle. Most rehabilitation regimes include physical exercise and what better way to exercise than sport?

There is an increase in obesity in the Western world due to our diets and lack of exercise. Embarrassment is a powerful emotion that prevents many people taking the step towards sport. There needs to be encouragement and the right environment for such people to be involved in sport. Joining clubs such as 'Weight Watchers' can encourage some to take exercise, which may lead to participation in a sport. Others would disagree and would find joining such an organisation demeaning and only reinforces individuals' lack of self-worth. This lack of self-esteem is an important factor and must be tackled for an individual to gain the confidence necessary to join others and participate in sport.

▲ Figure 3.1.2 There is an increase in obesity in the Western world due to our diets and lack of exercise

Much evidence points towards a real fall in the levels of participation by 16–19 year olds.

One particular study (Moran (2014) Sport and Exercise Psychology) sampled youth sport participants and found that while over a quarter of children were participating in sport at 10 years of age, this dropped significantly to just over 3 per cent at age 18. Females indicated that negative physical and emotional experiences in sport led to their decision to discontinue participation. Males suggested that the competitive nature of participation led to them giving up (especially if they lost in competition).

Gender

There are far more men than women who get involved in sport either to participate or to spectate. Some people still believe that being good at or interested in sport is somehow 'unfeminine', thus reinforcing male dominance in sport and sport coverage. Certain activities are traditionally linked to either males or females and this can lead to discrimination. For example, the funding for women's football is significantly lower than the funding for men's football in the UK.

Nevertheless, more women are now involved in physical exercise and there is far more interest in health and fitness matters. The participation rates for women in sports such as football and rugby continue to grow, there is an increase in the number of female sports presenters, which may encourage more women to take an interest in sport, and there are fewer instances of open discrimination against women participating in clubs such as golf clubs.

In spite of this progress, however, even now women's sport in the media is often covered because of what they look like rather than their achievements. For example, in newspapers, photographs of women tennis players with comments about their clothing is often at the detriment to discussion of their merits as players. Career earnings and media and television coverage for women severely lag behind.

IN THE NEWS

In 2013 the BBC presenter John Inverdale's comments about Wimbledon champion Marion Bartoli's personal appearance resulted in uproar. The BBC received almost 700 complaints in the hours after Inverdale, speaking on Radio 5 Live ahead of the game, said Bartoli 'was never going to be a looker'.

Inverdale apologised to Bartoli 'if' any offence was caused, but this was widely felt to be indicative of the fact that the sports presenter was not aware that his remark could only be interpreted as offensive.

While chatting on air about Bartoli's technique as a player, Inverdale said: 'I just wonder if her dad, because he has obviously been the most influential person in her life, did say to her when she was 12, 13, 14 maybe, "Listen, you are never going to be, you know, a looker. You are never going to be somebody like a Sharapova, you're never going to be 5 feet 11, you're never going to be somebody with long legs, so you have to compensate for that. You are going to have to be the most dogged, determined fighter that anyone has ever seen on the tennis court if you are going to make it." And she kind of is.'

Bartoli dismissed Inverdale's comments as irrelevant. She said later: 'It doesn't matter, honestly. I am not blonde, yes. That is a fact. Have I dreamt about having a model contract? No. I'm sorry. But have I dreamed about winning Wimbledon? Absolutely, yes. And to share this moment with my dad was absolutely amazing and I am so proud of it.'

? Extend your knowledge

London 2012 GB female medal tally

Christine Ohuruogu	400m (silver)
Jessica Ennis	Heptathlon (gold)
Nicola Adams	Flyweight boxing (gold)
Lizzie Armitstead	Road race (silver)
Victoria Pendleton	Sprint (silver)
Victoria Pendleton	Keirin (gold)
Laura Trott	Omnium (gold)
Dani King/Joanna Rowsell/Laura Trott	Team pursuit (gold)
Charlotte Dujardin	Individual dressage (gold)
Laura Bechtolsheimer	Individual dressage (bronze)
Charlotte Dujardin/Laura Bechtolsheimer/ (Carl Hester)	Team dressage (gold)
Zara Phillips/Mary King/Nicola Wilson/Kristina Cook/(William Fox-Pitt)	Team eventing (silver)
Beth Tweddle	Uneven bars (bronze)
Gemma Gibbons	Judo −78kg (silver)
Karina Bryant	Judo +78kg (bronze)
Helen Glover/Heather Stanning	Rowing women's pair (gold)
Anna Watkins/Katherine Grainger	Rowing double sculls (gold)
Katherine Copeland/Sophie Hosking	Rowing lightweight double sculls (gold)
Rebecca Adlington	400m freestyle (bronze)
Rebecca Adlington	800m freestyle (bronze)
Laura Robson/(Andy Murray)	Mixed doubles (silver)
Jade Jones	Taekwondo −57kg (gold)

▲ Figure 3.1.3 Women are regularly involved at the highest level in many sports previously dominated by men

> **STUDY HINT**
>
> Be prepared in exams to link data on participation rates with factors that are affecting those participation rates. For example, currently 40.6 per cent of men play sport at least once a week, compared with 30.7 per cent of women. At a younger age, men are much more likely than women to play sport. But this difference declines sharply with age.
>
> A possible exam question might be: Why are there about 10 per cent fewer females than males involved in sport?

Ethnicity, religion and culture

Some ethnic groups and religions may support physical activity and sport, or may have high regard for some activities rather than others, and these views may influence participation. Some cultures or religious beliefs may act as barriers for those who wish to participate.

Discrimination of any kind has no place in sport or any aspect of society, yet regrettably it may well be a factor that stops those from minority ethnic backgrounds from participating in sport. Some people from minority ethnic backgrounds may feel that they 'don't belong' in certain sports or sports clubs because of the actual or perceived prejudice that might be exhibited by other participants, officials or administrators.

IN THE NEWS

The lack of black football managers (stats based on 2015 figures – FA 2015) is stark and shows that many variables, including racial discrimination, are still a feature in sport.

- Of the 230 clubs that make up the seven tiers of English football below the top flight, only 14 have black managers (6.09 per cent). About 25 per cent of players in the Premier League and Football League are black. Based on current figures, only about 6.5 per cent of managers in the top four divisions – or six in 92 – are black.
- There are no black managers in the top four divisions of Scottish football. Or in Northern Ireland's top flight. As for Wales, Airbus UK's Andy Preece is the only black manager in the country's elite league.

Family

It is much more likely for you to be involved in sport if your parents or guardians participate themselves or promote the benefits of participation. Those whose families do not participate or who show little interest in sport are much less likely to be involved themselves.

Family support is often crucial for young people to be involved in higher levels of competition, with parents and guardians often having to transport and fund their children for sporting activities.

Parents, guardians and other significant members of the family can also make participation difficult through their own high or unrealistic expectations. Some family members put undue pressure on young people, who then become demotivated and disillusioned with sport and therefore give up or are unhappy when they compete.

IN THE NEWS

Reports in many newspapers in 2015 showed that parents supporting their children in football can become unruly, for example in *The Guardian* newspaper (12 September 2015):

What had been a Sunday morning under-15s football game had turned into a pitch invasion, then a full-scale scrap between two London teams. And their parents. 'Grown adults remonstrating with 15-year-olds on the pitch,' says James, the coach of one of the teams. 'The referee and linesmen were chased off the ground. It was crazy.' He doesn't quite know how it started – a player had been sent off, he thinks, and one of the parents made a comment – but tensions had been simmering between sets of parents all throughout the match. 'The kids got into an altercation with parents, then they retaliated, parents hitting kids, it was crazy. Full-on fisticuffs between 15-year-olds and grown men. Then the mums got involved, screaming and shouting.' The police turned up and made everyone go their separate ways.

Disability

More disabled people are taking part in sport, with the latest results showing more than 17 per cent in 2015 are playing sport regularly, up from about 15 per cent in 2005/6. Following the London 2012 Paralympic Games the participation levels have risen, but overall those with a disability show a comparatively low percentage in participation.

Those with a disability who wish to be involved in sport and physical activities face problems in getting access to facilities and may well feel discriminated against through this lack of suitable facilities and equipment. Some people with disabilities lack the confidence to get involved and also cannot find suitable activities that accommodate their disability and this results in a low rate of participation.

❓ Extend your knowledge

English Federation of Disability Sport (EFDS)

This is a national body that is responsible for developing sport for people with disabilities in England. It works closely with other national disability organisations recognised by Sport England:

- British Amputees and Les Autres Sports Association
- British Blind Sport
- British Deaf Sports Council
- British Wheelchair Sports Foundation
- Cerebral Palsy Sport
- Disability Sport England
- UK Sports Association for People with Learning Disability

The EFDS has a four-year national plan (2013–2017), 'Building a Fairer Sporting Society', which outlines the inclusion of disabled people in the identified national priority sports of athletics, boccia, cricket, football, goalball and swimming. It is also involved in the development of coach education and training opportunities, both of which are accessible to disabled people and cover the technical issues of coaching disabled people.

The objectives of the EFDS are:

- the creation of programmes for grass roots participation by disabled people
- to run a programme of events for disabled people
- the establishment of a talent identification system for disabled players and athletes
- the establishment of regional and national training squads for disabled players and athletes.

There are many reasons that people get involved in sport:

- Benefits to our health and fitness – sport can make us fitter and therefore healthier.
- Benefits to our well-being. Many people report that they feel better after participating in sport. It is accepted that certain hormones are released during exercise and that these can help us to feel more optimistic about life and better about ourselves.
- Benefits to manage stress. People often use sport as an escape from their working life. It has been recognised that by playing sport we can release some of our pent-up frustrations and aggressions – the squash ball can be hit hard to get rid of anger caused by frustrations at work or at school.
- Benefits to learning new skills – again giving a sense of accomplishment and also being able to compete eventually at a higher level and increasing our self-satisfaction when we overcome challenges and barriers.
- There is of course the huge benefit of meeting and participating with other people. New friends can be made through sport, which again is important for our sense of well-being.

Media coverage

The media and commercialisation will be dealt with in chapter 3.2. The media can play an important role in shaping attitudes to sports participation.

The type of sports that get the most media coverage is limited, with football getting the most. Male sport also still dominates, although there is a refreshing interest in women's football – for example, the ticket sales for the England versus Germany women's football comparative match in November 2014 outstripped those for the previous men's England friendly. This interest was also bolstered by the GB women's football comparative success in the 2012 Olympics when they reached the quarter finals of the competition.

The media can stimulate participation in sport. You only have to see the greater activity on municipal tennis courts during the Wimbledon fortnight to appreciate that watching sport can encourage participation. Our interest in playing a sport is particularly increased when the media highlights the success of UK sportspeople. There was a surge of interest in cycling, for instance, after success in the 2012 London Olympics when six world track records were achieved.

▲ Figure 3.1.4 Wimbledon fortnight can stimulate participation in tennis

STUDY HINT

To prepare for the examination it's helpful if you can learn a summary of how the media can affect participation in sport positively and negatively:

Positive:
- ✔ promotes or encourages sport and exercise, and increases interest through sports coverage
- ✔ promotes healthy living
- ✔ can motivate through role models
- ✔ promotional campaigns or public service broadcasting or through advertising
- ✔ provide a wide variety of sports, including minority and novel sports
- ✔ will create funds and sponsorship that can be used to encourage activity
- ✔ gives information about healthy lifestyles and fitness, e.g. via the internet or new training methods.

Negative:
- ✔ may encourage or reinforce unhealthy or inactive lifestyle
- ✔ may show negative role models
- ✔ too much passive watching and listening to media discourages activity, causing the 'couch potato' syndrome
- ✔ minority sports (those in which few people participate) are often under-represented
- ✔ women's sports are under-represented or misrepresented
- ✔ disability sport is under-represented or misrepresented
- ✔ older performers are often under-represented
- ✔ can make people feel inadequate by not having the ability or skill or the 'sporty' body image
- ✔ might show the dangers of participation or (high) risk of injury that might put people off participation.

Other possible reasons that people do not get involved in sport

- **Environment and climate**: this often dictates whether the activity can be indoors or outdoors and in some cases may well stop participation in a particular activity. Bringing down core body temperature is vital before, during and after exercise or competing. Ice jackets, wrist and feet cooling in tanks of cold water, and ice towels for the head and neck all help. Pinsent and Cracknell and the other rowers all did it, as well as the cyclists and even the GB women's hockey team. The English Institute of Sport researches other environmental factors such as pollution and the cold of winter games.
- **Time**: work commitments can get in the way of finding enough time for sport.
- **Resources**: you may or may not have appropriate facilities or sports clubs near to you. This can dictate whether you participate in sport or not. Some local authorities lay on a transport service for those who wish to visit a sports facility, for example the elderly may catch a specially run bus to a local leisure centre.
- **Role models**: like parents, other significant individuals can influence whether you participate in sport. If your peers are very sporty and they see sport as a worthwhile activity, then as a member of that peer group you too are more likely to participate. If those within your peer group do not take part in sport or have an anti-sport/fitness culture then you are less likely to participate.

▲ Figure 3.1.5 If your area of the country has regular snow then snow-based activities are more likely

Strategies to improve participation

The three important factors that can deliver successful strategies for improving participation are:
- promotion or convincing people they should take up sport
- provision of facilities, equipment, coaching etc.
- access, or giving people opportunity to participate by making it easier for them to engage in sport

The promotion, provision and access for sport are delivered by a number of agencies, such as UK Sport and Sport England, as well as government strategies to promote participation in sport.

Public, private and voluntary agencies

Public, private and voluntary agencies all promote sport in the UK. We all pay through our taxes to the government, which in turn funds public organisations. Private sector organisations include commercial businesses trying to make a profit and non-profit-making voluntary organisations such as the Youth Hostels Association or amateur sports clubs.

- Public facilities include local leisure centres, run by the local authority and funded via the taxpayer.
- Private facilities include local private health and fitness clubs.
- The voluntary sector facilities include local athletic clubs where you could train to keep fit. The Youth Hostels Association is another example of a voluntary organisation, which would give you information and concessionary rates to stay at youth hostels so that you can walk or ramble to keep fit.

▲ Figure 3.1.6 Sport is provided through public, private and voluntary agencies

The public sector includes local authorities (e.g. councils), which promote sport according to what they perceive to be the interests of the local population – for example, basketball to improve levels of participation and excellence and to improve basketball court facilities.

The private sector provides sport again according to local needs and often strives to get as many people involved as possible, to raise attendance levels and, importantly, because they are money-making organisations, to improve their profits. An example of a private club would be LA Fitness Health and Fitness Club, which provides the equipment, instruction in fitness activities and also, increasingly, personal training.

The voluntary sector aims to help provide support for local needs. It promotes specific sports, for example the local hockey club, which strives to get as many people to play hockey as possible and to attract men and women from all walks of life to the game. Such a club would run teams in local leagues and hold training sessions for its members.

Department for Culture, Media & Sport (DCMS)

This is a government department that has responsibility for government policy related to sport. The department has a minister associated with it who is responsible for sport.

UK Sport

The role of UK Sport, an agency under government direction, is to provide support for elite sportspeople who have a high level of performance or have the potential to reach the top. The organisation not only distributes government funds, including lottery money, but also supports world-class performers and promotes ethical standards of behaviour, including the fight against the use of performance-enhancing drugs through its anti-doping programme.

UK Sport oversees the work of sports councils in England, Scotland, Wales and Northern Ireland. These are:

- Sport England
- Sportscotland
- Sports Council for Northern Ireland
- Sports Council for Wales.

UK Sports Institute (UKSI)

The aim of this organisation is to provide the very best sportspeople with appropriate facilities and support. It offers sports science advice, coaching expertise and top training facilities. The UKSI comprises a number of centres located around the UK. Each individual sports council of England, Scotland, Wales and Northern Ireland has responsibility for the development of the UKSI in its area.

Youth Sports Trust (YST)

The YST is a sports agency responsible for the development of sport for young people. It has created a sporting pathway for all children through a series of linked schemes called the TOP programmes, aimed at encouraging young people from 18 months to 18 years to follow a healthy and active lifestyle.

Governing bodies

The majority of sports that we know today were developed and organised in the late 19th century. The participants needed to agree rules and regulations for their sports and so they met and formed committees called governing bodies – for example, the Football Association (FA), the Lawn Tennis Association (LTA), the Amateur Swimming Association (ASA), the Rugby Football Union (RFU), etc. There are more than 265 governing bodies in the UK. The teams and clubs pay a subscription to the governing body. They in turn administer the sport nationally and organise competitions and organise the national team. There are still many amateur positions within each governing body, but increasingly more salaried members of staff are involved.

The national governing bodies are also members of international governing bodies, for example Union des Associations Européennes de Football (UEFA) and Fédération Internationale de Football Association (FIFA). These international bodies control and organise international competitions.

> **? Extend your knowledge**
>
> UK Sport feels that its purpose is to lead the UK to sporting excellence by supporting winning athletes, world-class events and ethically fair and drug-free sport. UK Sport receives government funding in order to fulfil its role as the UK's national anti-doping agency, as well as funding a number of support programmes.

Methods of encouraging people into physical activity:

- ensuring that images and photos used illustrate the range of participants currently involved in the physical activity
- featuring in governing body publications, stories or articles that address the issue of equity within physical activity, from both positive and negative standpoints
- senior figures in the sport and physical activity making a public statement about their intention to tackle inequality issues
- allocating financial resources for physical activity.

Methods of encouraging disabled people into physical activity:

- promoting the inclusion of disabled people in the mainstream programmes of national governing bodies of sport, local authorities and other providers
- increasing funding
- raising the profile of physical activity and sport for disabled people.

For women in physical activity

Statistics reveal a number of inequalities, particularly in the higher levels of coaching and administration. Female athletes made up 40 per cent of the British team at the 1996 Olympic Games, yet only 11 per cent of coaches were women.

Active Communities

Active Communities is a 'framework' comprising services, products and sources of funding provided by Sport England, often in partnership with other organisations and agencies, to assist individuals and organisations to create their own Active Communities. The framework is organised under five core headings, which reflect the most important issues leading to the development of an Active Community:

- promoting social justice
- increasing participation in sport
- developing community sports leaders
- developing community sports programmes and facilities
- planning for sport and recreation.

Gender equity (equality)

To ensure that males and females are treated equally in sport, there are some principles that might lead to an increase in women's involvement and participation, including:

1. An increase in awareness of the issues surrounding women's and girls' involvement in physical activity.
2. Giving support to women and girls to become involved in physical activity at all levels and in all capacities.
3. Encouraging organisations to improve access to physical activity opportunities for women and girls.
4. Challenging instances of inequality found in physical activity and sport and seeking to bring about change.
5. Raising the visibility of all British sportswomen.

Other strategies for gender equity

- To provide gender awareness training for governing body coaches, leaders and organisers.
- To establish a programme of courses that will recruit women into the management of physical activity and sport.
- To raise the profile of women in officiating.

Government healthy living initiative

The government was prompted to act following a recognition of the barriers against healthy eating:

- limited parental awareness of weight status and associated health risks
- parental beliefs that a healthy lifestyle is too challenging
- pressures on parents that undermine healthy food choices
- a perception that there are limited opportunities for active lifestyles.

The government's healthy living programme aims to tackle these barriers through a range of initiatives aimed at families with young children. Young families are aware of the 5 A Day message but are not necessarily eating 5 A Day.

Top Tips for Top Mums

This is an extension of the highly successful 5 A Day campaign and encourages parents across the country to share tips and ideas on how they get their children to eat more fruit and vegetables. Top Tips for Top Mums targets young families from low-income backgrounds with children aged between 2 and 11. Recent research by the Food Standards Agency showed that only 46 per cent of people on lower incomes eat 5 A Day compared with 72 per cent of those on higher incomes.

5 A Day

Eating 5 A Day sets children up for a healthy lifestyle. Fruit and vegetables of different colours provide a wide range of vitamins, minerals, fibre and healthy antioxidants, which can help to protect the body throughout life. Research has shown that eating five or more a day can help a person to maintain a healthier diet. People who eat lots of fruit and vegetables can have a lower risk of heart disease, high blood pressure strokes and some cancers. To get the best benefit from the nutrients packed into fruit and vegetables, everyone should aim for a variety of types and colours every day.

Promotion of healthy diets and physical activity in the run-up to the 2012 Olympics

A collection of companies, including BSkyB, ITV, Tesco, Coca-Cola, Cadbury and AOL, pledged the equivalent of more than £200 million in advertising space and services to support the government's 'Change4Life' healthy lifestyles marketing initiative.

Change4Life

Change4Life is a movement, supported by the Department of Health, which aims to improve children's diets and levels of activity, thus reducing

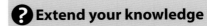

Extend your knowledge

There have been many government initiatives to promote healthy lifestyles. It is important to keep in touch with the latest developments and information can be found from the following sources:

- Local Government Association www.lga.gov.uk
- Active Places www.activeplaces.com
- UK Sport www.uksport.gov.uk
- Sport England www.sportengland.org
- Department for Culture, Media and Sport www.culture.gov.uk
- National Sports Foundation www.nationalsports foundation.org/

Other useful links:

- http://nds.coi.gov.uk/ environment/
- www.heartforum.org.uk
- www.skillsactive.com
- new.wales.gov.uk
- www.scotland.gov.uk
- www.patient.co.uk
- www.bhfactive.org.uk

the threat to their future health and happiness. The goal is to help every family in England eat well, move more and live longer.

Five choices to help you stay healthy

1. You should not smoke. Stopping smoking is often the single most effective thing that you can do to reduce your risk of future illness. The risk to health falls rapidly as soon as you stop smoking (but it takes a few years before the increased risk reduces completely).

2. Do some regular physical activity. Anything that gets you mildly out of breath and a little sweaty is fine – for example, jogging, heavy gardening, swimming, cycling, etc. A brisk walk each day is what many people do – and that is fine. However, it is thought that the more vigorous the activity, the better. To gain most benefit you should do at least 30 minutes of physical activity on most days. Two shorter bursts is thought to be just as good, for example two 15-minute bouts of activity at different times in a day.

3. Eat a healthy diet. Briefly, a healthy diet means:
   - At least five portions, and ideally 7–9 portions, of *a range of* fruit and vegetables per day.
   - The bulk of most meals should be starch-based foods (such as cereals, wholegrain bread, potatoes, rice, pasta), plus fruit and vegetables.
   - Not much fatty food such as fatty meats, cheeses, full-cream milk, fried food, butter, etc. Use low fat, mono- or poly-unsaturated spreads.
   - Include 2–3 portions of fish per week, at least one of which should be 'oily' (such as herring, mackerel, sardines, kippers, pilchards, salmon or *fresh* tuna).
   - If you eat meat it is best to eat lean meat, or poultry such as chicken.
   - If you do fry, choose a vegetable oil such as sunflower, rapeseed or olive oil.
   - Try not to add salt to food, and limit foods that are salty.

4. Try to lose weight if you are overweight or obese.
   - You don't need to get to a perfect weight.
   - If you are overweight you can gain great health benefits by losing 5–10 per cent of your weight.

5. Don't drink too much alcohol.
   - A small amount of alcohol is usually fine (for over 18 years only), but too much can be harmful. In fact, recent research from the UK Department of Health (January 2016) has identified that any level of consumption of alcohol is potentially harmful.
   - Men should drink no more than 21 units per week (and no more than 4 units in any one day).
   - Women should drink no more than 14 units per week (and no more than 3 units in any one day).
   - One unit is in about half a pint of normal-strength beer, or two thirds of a small glass of wine, or one small pub measure of spirits.

SUMMARY

- Target to increase participation is for people aged 14 and older taking part in sport for at least 30 minutes once a week.
- Participation in sport for at least 30 minutes a week has remained fairly steady over the last few years, at around 33 per cent of adults.
- The proportion of 16–24 year olds participating in sport has decreased (down from 76.8 per cent to 72.1 per cent).
- The most popular sports are walking (46 per cent), swimming (35 per cent), keep fit/yoga (22 per cent), cycling (19 per cent).
- Men are more likely than women to participate in sports activities – about 51 per cent of men compared with 36 per cent of women.
- The proportion of adults who take part in at least one sport or physical activity generally decreases with age.
- Relatively few people with a disability are involved in sport. Of those who take part, 89 per cent are from white British backgrounds.
- The rate of participation among people aged 16 years and over is greater in people from higher socio-economic groups than those from lower socio-economic groups.
- Following the London 2012 Paralympics the participation levels have risen, but overall those with a disability show a comparatively low percentage in participation.
- The promotion, provision and access for sport are delivered by a number of agencies, such as UK Sport and Sport England, as well as government strategies to promote participation in sport.

Practice questions

1. What are the main trends in sports participation for age and gender in the UK? **(6 marks)**
2. What three sports are the most popular in the UK and what are the main reasons for their popularity? **(8 marks)**
3. How can the family affect participation in sport? **(4 marks)**
4. Outline three strategies to improve participation in sport. **(6 marks)**

Chapter 3.2
Commercialisation of physical activity and sport

Understanding the Specification

You should understand the influence of the media on the commercialisation of physical activity and sport. You should know different types of media:

- social
- internet
- TV/visual
- newspapers/magazines.

You should know the meaning of commercialisation, including sport, sponsorship and the media (the golden triangle), and recognise the positive and negative effects of the media on commercialisation and be able to apply practical examples to these issues. Finally, you should understand the influence of sponsorship on the commercialisation of physical activity and sport, including the positive and negative effects of sponsorship on commercialisation and be able to apply practical examples to the issue of sponsorship.

Key term

Commercialisation This refers to the influence of commerce, trade or business on an industry (e.g. sport) to make a profit.

The influence of the media

This chapter looks at the **commercialisation** of physical activity and sport. Television companies spend an enormous amount of money on the broadcasting rights to sports-related events. To view certain events such as boxing the subscriber often needs to make an extra payment (pay-per-view). Sky, for example, holds the rights to many Premiership football games, which can be viewed only if you subscribe to a Sky package. Digital TV has also influenced sport – and not always to everyone's benefit. There has never before been so much coverage of sport on TV, but because of satellite TV dominating this coverage, only those who can afford to subscribe have access to many sports events. The terrestrial channels such as BBC and ITV have lost many of the major sports events and you get the ludicrous example of the BBC News unable to show a clip of a boxing match because the rights to that match are owned by another company.

The 'golden triangle' – sport, sponsorship and the media

This is the term used to show the interdependence and influences of the three factors of sport, sponsorship and the media. All these factors influence one another.

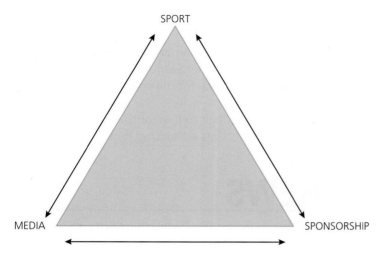

▲ Figure 3.2.1 The 'golden triangle'

Types of media are as follows:

- **Television**: BBC, ITV, Channel 4, Channel 5, satellite, cable, digital, factual/fiction/advertising.
- **Press**: broadsheets, tabloids, local, weekly, magazines, periodicals.
- **Radio**: national, local, commercial.
- **Internet**: including social media.
- **Cinema**: documentaries, movies (USA/UK/Bollywood, etc.).

Event programming has been revised because of the needs of the TV companies. Football fans, for instance, are finding that their team may play on a Sunday at 6pm, which has not traditionally been a time slot for the game. Olympic Games events are often scheduled at irregular times because of the demands of TV companies that are beaming the events around the world across different time zones.

The rules of sport have also been influenced by the media. For instance, in cricket the third umpire, in the form of a video replay analysis, has come into force, largely due to the influence of TV. There has been a similar development in rugby football. The armchair spectator can now see the event at every angle and the officials' decisions are laid bare for scrutiny, hence the need for new technology to aid the decision makers on and off the field of play.

The extent of media involvement has also influenced the amount of sponsorship and advertising revenue available to participants, clubs and other sports organisations. This has brought much welcomed money into sport, but some may argue that this has been to only a small number of participants in a small number of sports and may well have led to the decrease in participation in minority sports and other physical activities.

The influence of sponsorship

The influence of sponsorship on the development of physical activity and sport has been enormous over the last 20 years. The exercise and sport market is now big business, with large amounts of money being spent by commercial companies on sports' participants and events. For example, a company such as Adidas might sponsor a top-class tennis player to wear a particular style of training shoe. At the other end of the scale, a local hockey club might attract a small amount of money to go towards the first team kit.

STUDY HINT

Summarise the positive and negative effects of the media in preparation for the examination:

Positive:

- ✔ to provide a 'shop window' (helps to 'sell' or promote) for businesses and their products as well as the sports
- ✔ to provide more funds to sports and participants via advertising and sponsorship
- ✔ to make it exciting, entertaining and interesting and therefore more attractive to people to participate and support
- ✔ influences rules and times of play to make the sport more accessible, which in turn helps to sell goods.

Negative:

- ✔ can over-sensationalise the negative aspects of sport, e.g. poor behaviour
- ✔ can assert too much control over sport
- ✔ too few (mainly male) sports benefit
- ✔ under-representation of minority groups including those with disabilities.

There has also been a significant increase in sponsorship due to sports clothing being fashionable. Training shoes have seen a huge increase in sales, for instance. Many people who wear trainers would never dream of participating in sport! Nevertheless, commercial companies recognise that top sports stars can be fashion role models for the young and therefore use them in advertising campaigns.

Sports sponsorship is increasingly difficult to find for the 'middle-ranking sports', such as hockey – those sports that are neither hugely popular nor minority sports.

IN THE NEWS

A report presented to national governing bodies blames the current climate on sports' inability to attract sufficient media coverage. Sports sponsorship can be a vital ingredient in the financing of governing bodies' activities. Many sports, however, are unable to attract sponsors because they cannot get television coverage.

Companies will sponsor all different aspects of a sports team, event or individual, including:

- stadiums and grounds – new stands or grounds will often be named after the sponsor who has put money towards the development
- clothing – teams usually get a shirt sponsor and often individual players will get deals for footwear
- equipment – companies, usually one of those that manufacture the equipment, will often sponsor a player's equipment
- accommodation and transport – companies often offer free transport and accommodation to big teams so people see them using their company
- competitions – companies may sponsor an actual competition or league so then their name and logo appear on all of the products and information regarding the competition. Sometimes it's even named after the company (e.g. the Barclays Premier League).

▲ Figure 3.2.2 The Emirates Stadium, named after the international airline and team sponsor, is the home of Arsenal Football Club

Sponsorship in sport is good for many reasons:
- It provides money for athletes to train and compete full time.
- It often pays for competitions.
- It promotes the development of new athletes – sponsors offer scholarships and some universities and colleges offer places to students who excel at a sport for either lower grades or less in tuition fees so that the institution develops a good sporting reputation.
- It is good for the sponsors themselves:
  - They get free advertising – if you see the best players using a product, you might want to use it, too.
  - They get an attractive image – most sponsors want to be associated with winners.
  - They benefit through tax concessions and through providing hospitality for clients and business partners – sponsorship money isn't usually taxed. Company associates and athletes are also given free tickets in good viewing positions, often with food and drinks included, which they can use to impress possible clients and employees.

Sponsors often give money to charity events. This may be because they believe in a worthy cause. It may also be to help their image.

Sponsorship can also be negative:
- Companies don't want to sponsor teams and athletes who are not successful and so some struggle to get financial help this way.
- A narrow range of sports attracts most sponsors and therefore many sports miss out on useful funding.
- Sponsorship deals are fragile. For example, an injury, loss of form or some bad publicity can mean the contract is terminated and the sponsorship lost.
- Advertising some products in sport is not advisable. Advertising of cigarettes by tobacco companies has now been phased out in Formula One motor racing.

STUDY HINT
The main points regarding sponsorship to learn for the examination are as follows:
1. Sponsors continue to seek image enhancement and brand awareness through sponsorship and see this to be largely dependent on broadcast and other media coverage.
2. Sponsors are looking to sell their products, develop promotional opportunities and demonstrate that they are good corporate citizens.
3. Sponsors continue to be attracted to the 'top ten' sports and/or to community-based activity; 'middle-ranking' sports such as hockey are rarely considered.
4. Women's sport has the potential to attract more sponsors but to date most of that potential is unfulfilled.
5. Many sports are becoming more commercially aware, but some demonstrate naivety over valuing their rights and approaching sponsors.

❓ Extend your knowledge

Sports organisations have a number of other sources of funding, including grants, subsidies, membership fees and lottery funding:

- **Grants**. These are made available to public and voluntary sectors (more about these in a forthcoming chapter) usually. There is an increase in private sector projects being funded as long as the project benefits the local population and is gained from the government – local, national and the European Union. Buildings and equipment are typically funded by such bodies. Many grants involve the sports organisation putting forward a percentage of the funds themselves, for example 50 per cent government funds, 50 per cent of the costs funded by themselves.

- **Subsidies**. If the local authorities or councils tried to cover all the costs of sport, then few people would be able to participate, for example in swimming. Therefore there is a system of subsidies whereby members of the public pay a certain cost and the local authority pays the rest. Tax payers fund these subsidies via local government.

- **Membership fees**. All sports organisations with a membership – usually the voluntary sector – can take a significant proportion of their income from membership fees. For example, to join a hockey club each player pays an annual membership fee and often a 'match fee' for each game they play.

- **The National Lottery**. This is regarded as a grant for sport. World-class performers are also funded through the lottery. UK Sport is lottery funded and this in turn funds high-performance sport in the UK. Sport England, Sportscotland and Sport Wales are also lottery funds and these fund sport at all levels.

SUMMARY

- Different types of media include television, press (magazines/periodicals), radio, cinema, internet (including social media).
- The media has brought money into sport, but this has gone to only a small number of participants in a small number of sports and may well have led to the decrease in participation in minority sports and other physical activities.
- The 'golden triangle' is the term used to show the interdependence and influences of the three factors of sport, sponsorship and the media.
- The extent of media involvement has also influenced the amount of sponsorship and advertising revenue available to participants, clubs and other sports organisations.
- The exercise and sport market is now big business, with commercial companies spending large amounts of money on sports' participants and events.

Practice questions

1. Describe the influence of the media on the commercialism in sport.   (5 marks)
2. Give four different types of media and for each give an example of how sport is promoted.   (8 marks)
3. Describe the 'golden triangle' in sport.   (3 marks)
4. Discuss the positive and negative effects of sponsorship on the commercialisation of sport in the UK.   (10 marks)

Understanding the Specification

You should know the definitions of:

- sportsmanship
- gamesmanship
- deviance

and be able to apply practical examples to these concepts.

You should know the reasons why sports performers use drugs and the types of drugs and their effect on performance, with practical examples of these drugs in sport. You should also know the reasons for player violence and give practical examples of violence in sport.

Ethics and sport

Being ethical in sport is to play by the rules and to show high moral standards in your behaviour. Sport is supposed to be a fair activity, with everyone having an equal opportunity to apply their abilities in whatever activity they are performing. Three aspects that affect ethics in sport are sportsmanship, gamesmanship and deviance.

Sportsmanship

Sportsmanship involves fairness and generosity. Those who show good sportsmanship stick to the rules and regulations but also show that they can lose gracefully and with good humour.

If you compete in a physical activity it is often good to shake your opponent's hand before and after the event. If you accidentally hurt or injure an opponent you would show good sportsmanship by seeing that person's well-being as your priority rather than winning the game.

In exercise generally there are good manners in using facilities and equipment. For example, if you are working out in a gymnasium you return the free weights to the containing rack after you have used them. If you use exercise equipment then it is good manners or **etiquette** to towel down the machine you have used to remove your sweat.

Key terms

Sportsmanship This involves behaviour that shows fair play, respect for opponents and gracious behaviour, whether winning or losing.

Etiquette This is about the customs we observe surrounding the rules and regulations of the physical activity and also about what is socially acceptable in a particular culture. It involves a convention or an accepted way of behaving in a particular situation.

▲ Figure 3.3.1 Good sportsmanship makes for a pleasant and respectful environment

> **? Extend your knowledge**
>
> ### Sportsmanship associated with cricket
>
> Cricket has always been seen as the 'gentleman's game and that means there are certain traditions of the game that should be respected. Here are some examples of good etiquette:
>
> - **Walk when you're out**. Sadly this is a tradition that has gone out of the game at the highest level. But there will be times when you know you've got an edge through to the wicketkeeper that the umpire's missed. Whether you own up and walk is your decision, but it is regarded as good etiquette to walk.
> - **Umpire's decision is final**. Once a decision has been made, there's no turning back. So that means no arguing with the umpire.
> - **Applaud the new batsman**. No matter whether you're playing for your school or your country, it's good etiquette to clap the new batsman making their way to the wicket.

> **Activity**
>
> Choose a physical activity and then write a set of sportsmanship guidelines for that activity. Don't write about the actual rules but state what is acceptable and what is not as far as behaviour is concerned.

Other examples of good sportsmanship:

- Shake hands with your opponent.
- Thank anyone who has been participating with you or against you.
- Show concern for others, especially when they are injured or under stress.
- Never swear or be abusive.
- Do not stretch the rules to take advantage of someone else.
- Take defeat well and show good humour.
- Do not question officials – accept their decisions.
- Say 'well done' to opponents when they do well.
- Take other people into consideration when participating in exercise – for example, swimming and avoiding colliding with others.
- Do not over-celebrate when you do well – take other people's feelings into account and avoid arrogance in victory.
- Do not deride the efforts of others – be respectful of others, whatever their ability.

Gamesmanship

In many sports competitors are seen to 'bend the rules' or to put aside sportsmanship and use **gamesmanship** to seek an unfair advantage. There are those who may cheat within the sports competition but in a subtle way that is difficult to control by the rules. The forward in football who dives in the penalty area to seek a penalty, the hockey player who impedes another's stick in a tackle, an athlete who pushes another in a middle-distance race – these are all examples of gamesmanship that most people perceive to be undesirable elements in the sport. Often coaches are guilty of encouraging such behaviour and thus reinforcing the view that gamesmanship is a clever way of undermining your opponent and gaining an advantage in competition.

Key term

Gamesmanship The use of unethical, although often not illegal, methods to win or gain a serious advantage in a game or sport.

IN THE NEWS

Examples of gamesmanship that have been in the news:
- Diego Maradona's 'Hand of God' against England in the 1986 World Cup.
- Michael Schumacher deliberately taking out Damon Hill in the final race of the 1994 F1 championship.

Key term

Deviance This involves human behaviour that is against your society's norms and values. Behaviour of this kind is often against the law.

Deviance

There is a view that sport may well contribute to **deviance** in our society. Spectators at a sports event may be stirred to commit criminal acts by the sports spectacle. Some have the view that contact sports such as boxing or some martial arts may encourage violence and anti-social behaviour.

There are competitors in sport who use performance-enhancing drugs, which is of course against the rules. The pressure of trying to win and to have that all-important edge over your opponent drives some sportspeople to take drugs to help their performance or to enable them to train more effectively. Competitors' behaviour within a sports event can also be seen as deviant.

▲ Figure 3.3.2 Some people believe contact sports encourage anti-social behaviour

Other examples of deviance:
- Hooliganism in football.
- Violence in sports (e.g. a fight between players in a rugby match).
- Taking performance-enhancing drugs.
- Cheating in sports such as golf.

Drugs in sport

Sportspeople often take drugs to enhance their performance. Many feel that 'others are taking them, so why shouldn't I?' Others are influenced by peers or over-competitive coaches who seek winning by any means.

The use of drugs, whether they be recreational – for example, cannabis – or performance enhancing – for example, anabolic steroids – is widespread and can seriously affect your health and well-being. Drug taking involves the use of chemicals that alter the way we feel and see things and is one of the oldest activities of the human race.

Even when there are serious consequences to their use – of tobacco, alcohol, cannabis, heroin or performing-enhancing drugs in sport – those consequences will not always make a person want to stop using their drug of choice. If and when they do decide to give up, they may find it is harder than they thought. There is often more to an addiction than the physical withdrawal symptoms. Addiction includes anxiety, depression and lowering of self-esteem. The pattern of these symptoms will depend not only on the drug used but also on the psychological make-up of the person and the circumstances in which they are attempting to remain drug-free.

UK Sport has been directed by the government to deliver its policy objectives as the national anti-doping organisation, to represent the government in international meetings and to co-ordinate the national anti-doping programme of testing and education and information for sport throughout the UK.

Prohibited substances in sport

Prohibited substances may vary from sport to sport. It is the athlete's responsibility to know their sport's anti-doping regulations. In cases of uncertainty, it is important to check with the appropriate governing body or UK Sport and be sure to read carefully the anti-doping rules adopted by the relevant governing body and international sports federations.

Athletes are advised to check all medications and substances with their doctor or governing body medical officer. All substances should be checked carefully when travelling abroad as many products can, and do, contain substances different to those found in the UK.

Substances and methods are prohibited in sport for various reasons, including:

- Performance-enhancing effects, which contravene the ethics of sport and undermine the principles of fair participation.
- Health and safety of the athlete – some drug misuse may cause serious side effects, which can compromise an athlete's health. Using substances to mask pain/injury could make an injury worse or cause permanent damage. Some drug misuse may be harmful to other athletes participating in the sport.
- Illegality – it is forbidden by law to possess or supply some substances.

Most sporting federations have anti-doping regulations to ensure all athletes compete by the same principle of being drug-free. The regulations aim to achieve drug-free sport through clearly stated policies, testing and sanctions. They are also intended to raise the awareness of drug misuse and to deter athletes from misusing prohibited drugs and methods. Examples of performance-enhancing drugs include:

- **Anabolic steroids**: these enable sportspeople to train harder and longer and often lead to them increasing their strength and aggression.
- **Beta blockers**: these help to control the heart rate and keep the athlete calm.
- **Stimulants**: for example, amphetamines – these work as a brain stimulant, which increases alertness.

❓ Extend your knowledge

Anabolic steroids

These are man-made drugs that increase muscle growth if taken with vigorous training. This enables the athlete to recover more quickly and therefore to be able to train even harder.

The main problems with taking such drugs are:

- both the liver and the kidneys can develop tumours
- the liver ceases to act properly, causing major health problems
- high blood pressure, severe acne or spots
- shrinking of the testicles, reduced sperm count and the development of breasts in males
- the growth of facial hair, baldness and deepening of the voice in females.

There is also an increase in aggression and other psychological problems.

❓ Extend your knowledge

Prohibited classes of substances

- Stimulants
- Narcotic analgesics
- Anabolic agents
- Anabolic androgenic steroids
- Other anabolic agents
- Diuretics
- Peptide hormones, mimetics and analogues
- Substances with anti-oestrogenic activity
- Masking agents

Prohibited methods

- Enhancement of oxygen transfer
- Blood doping
- The administration of products that enhance the uptake, transport and delivery of oxygen
- Pharmacological, chemical and physical manipulation
- Gene doping (to alter our genetic make-up, in order to make us stronger or faster)

Classes of prohibited substances in certain circumstances

- Alcohol
- Cannabinoids
- Local anaesthetics
- Glucocorticosteroids
- Beta blockers

IN THE NEWS

In 2015 leaked IAAF (International Association of Athletics Federations) doping files caused alarm, especially with the World Anti-Doping Agency (Wada). According to media reports, the files pointed to an 'extraordinary extent of cheating' by athletes at the world's biggest events. Revelations allegedly reveal:

- A third of medals (146, including 55 golds) in endurance events at the Olympics and World Championships between 2001 and 2012 were won by athletes who recorded suspicious tests.
- More than 800 athletes (one in seven of those named in the files) have recorded blood tests described by one of the experts as 'highly suggestive of doping or at the very least abnormal'.
- British athletes, including Olympic champion heptathlete Jessica Ennis-Hill, have lost out in major events to competitors who were under suspicion.
- Ten medals at London 2012 were won by athletes who had dubious test results.
- Athletes are increasingly using blood transfusions and erythropoietin (EPO) micro-doses to boost their red cell count.

The evidence is not proof of doping, but the revelations will raise more serious questions over whether the sport is doing enough to combat cheating.

> **STUDY HINT**
> Be able to describe the positive and negative effects of performance-enhancing drugs:
> - ✔ **Positive**: able to play better/perform better/more strength/more aggressive/more energy available/control of emotions/able to train harder and longer.
> - ✔ **Negative**: jeopardising health/skin problems, e.g. acne/become addicted/high blood pressure/too aggressive/less self-esteem/masks injury/decreased speed/disqualification/loss of respect from others/gives a bad reputation to the individual and the sport.

IN THE NEWS

Drugs, deviance and making irretrievable mistakes

After six weeks of deliberation, the Court of Arbitration for Sport (CAS) in October 2002 decided to confirm the International Olympic Committee's (IOC) decision to disqualify Alain Baxter from the men's alpine skiing slalom event at the Salt Lake City Winter Games. Baxter finished third in the slalom and was awarded the bronze medal, but a subsequent doping test revealed traces of methamphetamine – a stimulant on the IOC's list of prohibited substances – in his urine sample.

Though Baxter maintained that the US Vicks nasal inhaler he used prior to the slalom race contained levmetamfetamine – a non-performance-enhancing isomer of methamphetamine – the CAS ruled that the anti-doping code of the Olympic movement prohibits all forms of methamphetamine and the presence of any prohibited substance results in automatic disqualification, whether or not ingestion was intentional.

Baxter now falls under the British Olympic Association's doping byelaw, which states that any athlete found guilty of a doping offence is ineligible to represent Great Britain at any future Olympic Games.

Violence in sport

The word violence is used frequently and in sport it is often used with the intent to harm others outside the rules of the game or activity. In sport it is often difficult to distinguish between what is violent and aggressive behaviour and what is not. A foul in rugby may look aggressive, but it could have been unintentional or an accident. Also, what is seemingly accidental on the surface may well have the intent to harm and therefore is aggression.

Possible reasons for player violence

Player violence unfortunately occurs in a number of sports and can lead to injuries to instigator and victim. There are many possible causes of player violence that you need to consider:

1. **We can't help it – it is an instinctive response.** This is known as the instinct theory. In sport we may have the instinctive urge to strike out and protect ourselves or to defend our territory. For example, in rugby a player in an offside position may well cause an opponent to be aggressive.

▲ Figure 3.3.3 In sport we may have the instinctive urge to strike out and protect ourselves or to defend our territory

2. **We get frustrated.** Again this is a type of instinct – if we feel frustrated we may well lash out and be aggressive to get rid of the frustration. Such things as playing poorly, or what we feel are poor decisions on the part of the referee, can cause frustration.

3. **We copy others.** To fit into a group and be accepted and to behave in a way that our role models do, we may become aggressive. If someone you look up to behaves aggressively you are more likely to imitate or copy their behaviour because you think that must be the right thing to do.

4. **We simply get angry.** This might be the result of frustration, as we have already explored, or you may have seen someone else get away with aggressive behaviour and not been punished. When we get angry our heart rate increases as well as our blood pressure and the hormone adrenaline is released more readily into the blood stream. We therefore get agitated and we want to show that we are angry and are therefore aggressive.

❓ Extend your knowledge

Strategies to control violence or aggression

The following strategies could be employed to control violence.

1. Calm down by relaxing or by concentrating on your own performance in the game or activity. Focusing attention on the job in hand is sometimes called channelling aggression.
2. Avoid situations that might make you angry or aggressive – for example, by walking away from trouble or trying a new position on the field of play.
3. Remove yourself completely from the situation – for instance, a basketball coach may substitute an aggressive player to calm down.
4. Enjoy praise for not being aggressive. Your coach may well praise the fact that you have been a forceful, effective player, but you have not been aggressive and given away territory.
5. Recognise others who are successful (role models) but who do not resort to aggression. Most successful sportspeople are not aggressive but are assertive.
6. Punishment or fear of being punished may well control aggression. Often fines are used or a player may be dropped from the team.
7. Recognise that you have a position of responsibility. Aggression could let the rest of the team down.
8. Anger management. Try to identify what makes you angry and to avoid the triggers to anger. You may learn to deal with your feelings early on rather than waiting for your anger to build up out of control.
9. Breathing exercises. Relax in your mind and body with deep, controlled and slow breathing. This can affect your heart rate, which will decrease the steadier your breathing, and then you will be able to feel calmer.

SUMMARY

- Ethics in sport include the concepts of sportsmanship, gamesmanship and deviance.
- Sportsmanship involves fairness and generosity.
- In many sports competitors are seen to 'bend the rules' or to put aside sportsmanship and use 'gamesmanship' to seek an unfair advantage.
- Deviance involves human behaviour that is against your society's norms and values.
- Anabolic steroids enable sportspeople to train harder and longer.
- Beta blockers help to control the heart rate and keep the athlete calm.
- Stimulants work to increase alertness for sportspeople.
- The word violence is used in sport as behaviour with the intent to harm others outside the rules of the game or activity. Violence is often used to get an advantage, to retaliate or because of a player's frustration.

Practice questions

1. It is recognised that participating in physical activities should be played showing sportsmanship. Which of the following is an example of sportsmanship when performing a physical activity?   **(1 mark)**
   a. Shaking hands with your opponent at the end of a tennis match.
   b. Obeying the referee in football.
   c. Shouting 'well played' to one of your team-mates in hockey.
   d. Politely questioning a decision made by the referee in basketball.

2. In an activity or your choice describe how good sportsmanship might be displayed by a participant.
                                                            (3 marks)

3. Define deviance in sport.   **(2 marks)**

4. Describe the effects of anabolic steroids on the sports performer.   **(3 marks)**

5. Discuss the reasons why sportspeople take performance-enhancing drugs.   **(10 marks)**

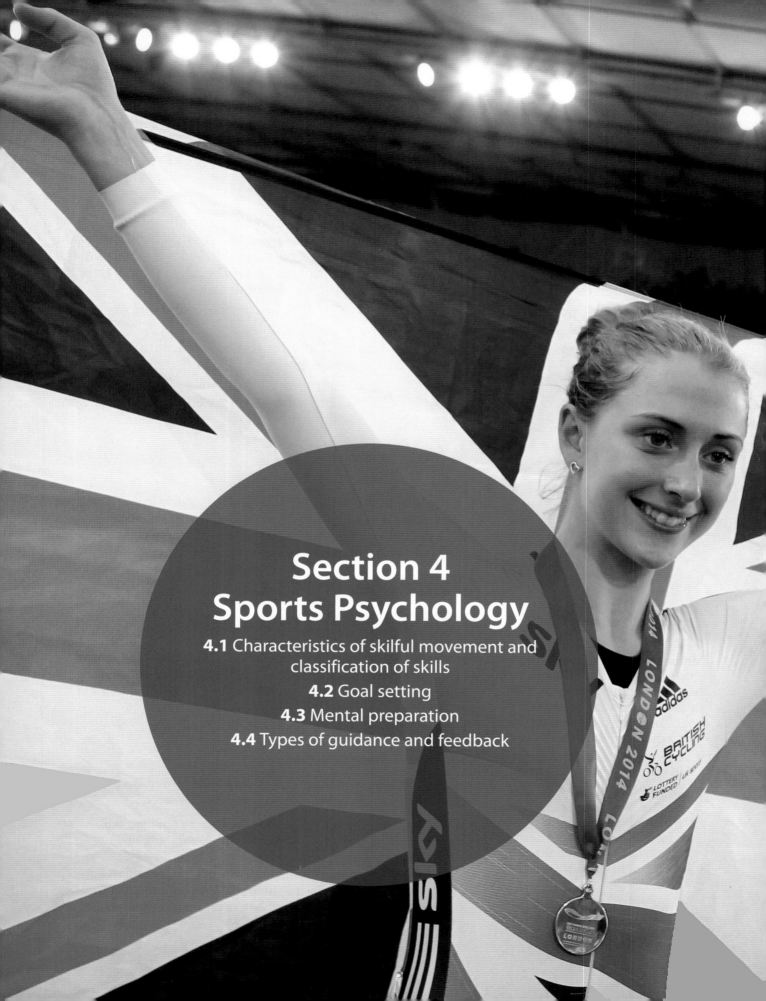

Section 4
Sports Psychology

4.1 Characteristics of skilful movement and
classification of skills

4.2 Goal setting

4.3 Mental preparation

4.4 Types of guidance and feedback

Chapter 4.1
Characteristics of skilful movement and classification of skills

Understanding the Specification

You should have knowledge and understanding of the characteristics of skilful movement when performing physical activities and sports and be able to apply them to practical examples.

- Definition of motor skills.
- Characteristics of skilled performers with a range of practical examples.
  - Efficiency
  - Pre-determined
  - Co-ordinated
  - Fluent
  - Aesthetic

You should also have knowledge and understanding of the identified classification of skills in both the learning and improvement of physical skills and be able to apply them to practical examples.

- The difficulty continuum from simple to complex skills.
- The environmental continuum from open to closed skills.
- Examples of skills for each continuum along with justification of their placement on both continua.

To strive to become good at your sport and to be skilful in everything you do, it is useful to be able to picture and describe what skilful movement actually is. We can then compare what we do with this picture of expertise and identify what we have to work on to improve.

Characteristics of skilled performers

When we use the term skill, we often mean a combination of perceptual (how we see our surroundings), cognitive (thinking skills) and **motor skills**. Skilled performers are not born with most motor skills already programmed in their minds – they have to learn them in a number of different ways.

Skilful movement

Skilful movement can be defined as:

A skilled movement is one in which a predetermined objective is accomplished with maximum efficiency with a minimum outlay of energy.

Are skilful people born with their skills or do they learn their skills? The answer is probably a mixture of both. We are all born with abilities and these dictate the potential to be skilful.

We often comment that an experienced sportsperson is 'skilful', but what do we actually mean by the word 'skill'? We use it to describe a task such as kicking a ball, but often we use it to mean the overall actions of someone who is good at what they do.

Key term

Motor skill An action or task that has a target or goal and that requires voluntary body and/or limb movement to achieve this goal. There are two main ways of using the word 'skill':

a. To see skill as a specific task to be performed.

b. To view skill as describing the quality of a particular action, which might include how consistent the performance is and how prepared the performer is to carry out the task.

When we see top-class sportsmen and sportswomen we are often struck by the seemingly effortless way in which they perform, and it is not until we try to perform ourselves that we realise just how difficult it really is! We know that these performers are very fit, but they don't seem to exert themselves and we are aware that whatever the skill – whether it is a somersault in gymnastics or a perfectly timed rugby tackle – the end product looks good and is aesthetically pleasing. A skilled performer knows what they are trying to achieve and shows a successful movement. A beginner, or novice, will seem clumsy and slow and will lack control. The novice will also tire quickly and use up more energy than is necessary. Characteristics of skilful movement include the movement being fluent, co-ordinated and controlled. The performer seems effortless and looks good, obviously using good technique.

IN THE NEWS

▲ Figure 4.1.2 Gymnast Kelly Simm

The Commonwealth gold medallist and Team GB gymnast Kelly Simm planned to perform a skill at the 2015 European Games that had never been used before. 'It could get named after me if I complete it, which is really exciting.'

Britain's top gymnast Beth Tweddle has had a gymnastic skill named after her. Beth is an excellent role model for her contemporaries.

Activity

▲ Figure 4.1.1 Lionel Messi: a skilled performer?

Look at the photograph. We would probably all agree that this performer is skilled. Write a list of words and phrases you feel would describe a skilled performer.

Skilful movement, then, is not one that can be described in one specific way, but is a mixture of features that when combined provides movement patterns that are effective and efficient.

Main characteristics with practical examples

- Efficiency, e.g. no wasted energy when hitting a ball in cricket.
- Pre-determined, e.g. the trampolinist knows her routine well before she starts.
- Co-ordinated, e.g. the volleyball player can jump and 'spike' successfully.
- Fluent, e.g. the rugby player picks up the ball and passes in one flowing movement.
- Aesthetic, e.g. the basketball player shoots the ball using the correct technique that looks good.

❓ Extend your knowledge

Other characteristics associated with skilled performers

The following is a list of other characteristics of skilled performers, together with examples:

- Creative, e.g. a rugby player can disguise a pass.
- Successful technique, e.g. a netball player shows the correct shooting technique.
- Controlled, e.g. a tennis player controls a smash that goes in.
- Speed, e.g. a lacrosse player passes with speed.
- Consistent, e.g. a squash player serves well every time.
- Well learned, e.g. a gymnast learns a new technique of somersault.
- Confident, e.g. a hockey player shows confidence when shooting at goal.

❓ Extend your knowledge

Fundamental motor skills

Skills such as throwing a ball or jumping or kicking a ball – we learn these skills at a young age, usually through play, and if they are learned thoroughly, a child can move on to the more sophisticated actions that are required in sport. When an accomplished hockey player, for instance, performs a skilful pass, they show a technically good movement. This movement is called the motor skill. Fundamental motor skills are skills such as throwing, catching and running. These skills are important because they provide the basis for other skills. Without acquiring the fundamental motor skills, it is unlikely that a person would be able to excel in a sports activity. These skills provide the platform on which we can build the more advanced skills demanded in our sports. Acquisition of these essential skills also helps us to follow a lifestyle that is healthy. As we get older, we may draw on many fundamental motor skills to play lifetime sports, such as golf. Acquiring fundamental motor skills can help children build their self-esteem and make them more accepted in group 'play' situations.

Key terms

Perception A complex concept that involves interpretation of stimuli. Not all stimuli are perceived and what is perceived depends on experience and attention ability.

Cognitive skills These are skills that involve the intellectual ability of the performer. These skills affect the perceptual process and help us to make sense of what is required in any given situation. They are essential if the performer is to make correct and effective decisions.

If a tennis player often serves aces in a match, we would label that player as skilled. If we watched him over a number of matches and he continued to serve aces, we would be more justified in labelling him as skilled. A squash player whom we might regard as skilled would anticipate where the ball is going to land and would put herself in a position to receive the ball early so that she could hit it early, thus putting her opponent at a disadvantage. The player also has to assess the position of the opponents and the players on the same team and will have to decide where to pass the ball and how hard to pass it. This interpretation of information or stimuli is called **perception** and the skill required is called *perceptual skill.*

For skill acquisition to take place the person also needs **cognitive skills**. These skills are intellectually based and are linked to working out or solving problems; they underpin verbal reasoning. These skills are often seen as innate, although there is considerable debate among psychologists as to how intelligence is acquired and whether there is only one or many ways that people can show intelligence.

Classification of skills

For the nature of skills to be understood fully and for those that teach and learn skills in sport, it is helpful to classify them. Classification makes it clearer about what is required to learn and perform a particular skill. Skills can be placed on a continuum or scale and for GCSE Physical Education the two continua that you need to be concerned with are:

- environmental continuum
- difficulty continuum.

If a skill is affected by the surrounding environment and requires the performer to make perceptual decisions, it is called an open skill. If a skill at the other extreme is not affected at all by the environment, it is called a closed skill.

Skills can be classified according to the types of judgements and decisions that you have to make to perform the skill. If there are many decisions to make, then the skill is known as a complex skill and may have to be learned in stages. If the skill is a straightforward one with hardly any judgements and decisions to make, then it is known as a simple skill and can be taught as a whole and in a fairly repetitive way.

Practical examples:

- complex skills – slip catch in cricket, or a pass by a midfield player in hockey who has to make lots of decisions before she passes
- simple skills – a sprint start in swimming, for example, where there are very few decisions – other than to dive – to be made.

▲ Figure 4.1.3 A slip catch in cricket is an example of a complex skill

Implications for training and coaching

If a coach and the performer are familiar with and understand the nature of the task or skill that has to be learned and performed, then training techniques can be adapted depending on these requirements.

If a closed skill is to be coached, it is going to be more effective if it is practised repetitively so that the skill is 'grooved'. It is also unnecessary to vary the situation because closed skills remain mainly constant. If an open

Activity

Your physical activity, sport or exercise programme will require fundamental motor skills, more advanced motor skills and perceptual skills. Identify:

a. the fundamental skills involved
b. the motor skills involved
c. any perceptual skills involved.

skill were learned then a variety of situations would be effective because the performer would build up a repertoire of strategies due to the ever-changing circumstances.

> ## SUMMARY
> - The main characteristics of skilled movement are learned, goal directed, predetermined goals, consistent achievement, economy of movement, efficiency, co-ordinated, precise, aesthetically pleasing, fluent, controlled.
> - Motor skills involve fundamental movement patterns and perceptual and cognitive skills.
> - If a skill is affected by the surrounding environment and requires the performer to make perceptual decisions, it is called an open skill. If a skill at the other extreme is not affected at all by the environment, it is called a closed skill.
> - Skills can be classified according to the types of judgements and amount of decisions that you have to make to perform the skill. If there are many decisions to make, the skill is known as a complex skill and may have to be learned in stages.
> - If the skill is a straightforward one with hardly any judgements and decisions to make, it is known as a simple skill and can be taught as a whole and in a fairly repetitive way.

Practice questions

1. Using practical examples, describe what is meant by a closed skill and a simple skill. **(2 marks)**

2. Which one of the following is the best example of a skilled performer in sport showing a predetermined characteristic? **(1 mark)**
   a. A gymnast performing a somersault in her floor routine.
   b. A rugby player assessing how well she has tackled an opponent.
   c. A tennis player deciding to serve to his opponent's backhand side.
   d. An athlete winning a 100 metre race.

3. Choosing a motor skill in sport, justify your classification of this skill on the environmental continuum. **(3 marks)**

Chapter 4.2
Goal setting

Understanding the Specification

You should understand and be able to apply examples of the use of goal setting for the following reasons:

- for exercise and training adherence
- to motivate performers
- to improve and optimise performance.

Candidates should also be able to understand the 'SMART principle' (Specific, Measurable, Achievable, Recorded, Timed) of goal setting with practical examples.

They should be able to apply the SMART principle, using practical examples to improve and optimise performance.

Goal setting

There are many reasons why goal setting can be important, including to encourage individuals to stick to a routine and to motivate performers. One common way of doing this is through the SMART principle. SMART stands for:

- Specific
- Measurable
- Achievable
- Recorded
- Timed

For exercise and training adherence

Goal setting has been shown as an effective method in ensuring that those people who wish to exercise or train to improve fitness, health and performance are more likely to stick to their exercise/training programmes. Too many goals can be irrelevant to the performer or can result in them giving up too quickly. Goals that are simply out of reach, too difficult or too demanding can result in a high dropout rate.

To motivate performers

Goal setting can inspire and drive performers to achieve their best and can be useful in motivating them to follow exercise and training programmes. But in order to motivate goals must follow the SMART principle and also be exciting and realistic. All performers, whether they are elite athletes striving for world records or are simply exercising to keep fit, are often motivated by short-term goals, leading to long-term goals. If goals or targets are reached each step of the way then performers are more likely to continue and to try their best to reach the next step towards further goals.

To improve and optimise performance

Goals that follow the SMART principle often lead to higher levels of performance, but goals should be incrementally more difficult over a period of time. Improvements can be seen only if each short-term goal is realistic but challenging. Goals set might lead to a decline in performance if they are set beyond the reach of the performer and this can also lead to demotivation and may result in the performer giving up altogether.

For goals to result in exercise adherence, motivated performers and improved performance, they need to be appropriate to performer's needs. By setting appropriate goals you can:

- take up an activity or activities
- achieve more when you participate in physical activities
- improve your performance
- improve the quality and quantity of your training
- increase your motivation to succeed
- increase your pride and satisfaction after goal completion.

Goal setting is a very powerful process that can lead to rewards, personal satisfaction and increased motivation levels. By knowing what you want to achieve, you then know what you need to concentrate on and improve and what distractions to ignore.

When you set goals for training in sport, you should try to:

- pace yourself – do not try to do too much too soon
- give yourself rewards
- keep goals realistic
- keep a record of your goals
- not feel bad if things do not go well – plan your next step for future success.

Achieving goals

When you have achieved a goal, enjoy the satisfaction of having done it – pat yourself on the back. Plan to achieve even greater or higher goals.

If you have failed to reach a goal, make sure that you have learned lessons from it to keep motivated and focused.

▲ Figure 4.2.1 Achieving a goal can lead to high levels of satisfaction

Reasons for not attaining goals in physical activities

- You did not try hard enough.
- Poor technique which needs to be adjusted.
- The goal you set was unrealistic at this time.

Use this information to adjust your goals or to set different goals to learn new skills or build to improve fitness. Turn everything into a positive learning experience. Failing to meet a goal is a step forward towards success.

When you have achieved a goal:

- if easily achieved, make your next goals harder
- if the goal took too long to achieve, make the next goals a little easier
- if you learned something that would lead you to change future goals, then change them.

Effective goal setting

For goal setting to be effective there must be short-term goals leading to longer-term goals. For example, to win the league cup, the netball team may have to concentrate on winning more games away from home. For this there may be short-term goals of improving the team's defending strategies. For those who simply wish to exercise more, the first step is to walk to school rather than any long-distance running.

Motivation can be increased by splitting long-term goals into medium-term and short-term goals, which are more specific and manageable over a short period of time.

People who exercise and sports performers need to know how they are progressing. Most sportspeople are highly motivated and feedback is essential for them to maintain their enthusiasm and commitment. For those who are exercising to keep fit, positive feedback is also crucial if they are going to keep exercising. Too many people join gyms in this country but stop going after the first few times.

❓ Extend your knowledge

Evaluation of goal setting

Goal evaluation must take place if progress is to be made and performance improved or participation increased. Goals must therefore be clearly defined. This is easier with physical activities and sports that involve objective measurements, e.g. times. Evaluation can take place only if goals are measurable. The measurement of goals will then give information about success, which in itself is a motivating factor and will also give useful information about the setting of further goals.

STUDY HINT

SMART goal setting

Be able to identify each element and then be able to apply each using a practical example, e.g. a specific goal to improve the serve technique in tennis.

S   Specific: if goals are clear and unambiguous they are more likely to be attained.

M   Measurable: this is important for monitoring and makes you accountable.

A   Achievable: motivation will improve if goals can actually be reached and are within your capabilities.

R   Recorded: crucial for monitoring and once achieved can be deleted or checked off, thus improving motivation.

T   Timed: the splitting up into short-term goals that are planned and progressive is effective.

▲ Figure 4.2.2 Goal setting is a useful strategy to control anxiety and one that is widely used in sport for training and to improve performance

IN THE NEWS

- There has been a sharp decline in the number of people joining gyms over the last few years – 54,000 fewer people now take out gym membership each year. For some people the gym has been pushed aside by yoga, Pilates and outdoor boot camp-style programmes such as 'military fitness circuits'.
- Almost a quarter of British adults are judged obese and, if current trends continue, 60 per cent of men and 50 per cent of women will be clinically obese by 2050.
- Yoga and Pilates studios are on the increase, more people are running now than during the jogging boom of the 1980s, and participation in activities as varied as ballroom dancing, ice-skating and triathlons is rising. It has become obvious to many people that there are other, more appealing, means of burning calories – and that even walking the dog or cycling to work can be considered good exercise.

If people exercise simply to lose weight, not because they enjoy it, they will either give up before they achieve their goal or will think 'job done' when it is finally reached, then revert to their old habits of inactivity.

Many surveys have indicated that six months after joining, the dropout rate among new gym members is about 60 per cent. One report suggested that 20 per cent of health club members work out there no more than once a month.

❓ Extend your knowledge

Performance and outcome goals

There are two types of goal that can be recognised and set in sport: performance and outcome goals.

Performance goals

These are directly related to the performance or technique of the activity. For example, performance goals in netball or football might be to improve passing or shooting techniques. Performance goals by their nature tend to be more short term than long term.

Examples of performance goals:

- To improve technique of a front somersault in trampolining.
- To try to stop using a poor golf swing when driving from the tee.
- To improve running technique in sprinting.
- To shorten the back swing in a tennis serve in order to be more accurate.
- To not let lifting technique go wrong when training with heavier weights.

Outcome goals

These are concerned with the end result, whether you win or lose for instance. Outcome goals in netball or football might be to win an individual game or a tournament. A tennis player who is trying to win the grand slam by winning each open tournament is setting another outcome goal. Outcome goals tend to be medium to long term rather than short term.

Examples of outcome goals:

- To win the 100 metre race in an athletics competition.
- To finish the exercise class without stopping.
- To try to draw level in a cycling race.
- To win the football league.
- To get through to the finals of the golf competition.

▲ Figure 4.2.3 A performance goal in netball might be to improve passing technique

Practice questions

1. Explain the SMART principle of goal setting and describe why goal setting is important for an active, healthy lifestyle. **(6 marks)**

2. Which one of the following is a valid reason for setting goals? **(1 mark)**
   a. To try to keep to an exercise programme
   b. To try to be lucky in a match
   c. To decrease self-esteem
   d. To reduce skill levels

3. SMART target setting is often used to improve performance in physical activities. Which one of the following does the **S** in the SMART principle stand for? **(1 mark)**
   a. Superficial
   b. Standardised
   c. Specific
   d. Special

SUMMARY

- For goals to result in exercise adherence, motivated performers and improved performance they need to be appropriate to the performer's needs.

- Goal setting is a very powerful process that can lead to rewards, personal satisfaction and increased motivation levels. By knowing what you want to achieve, you then know what you need to concentrate on and improve and what distractions to ignore.

- SMART stands for: Specific, Measurable, Achievable, Recorded, Timed.

Chapter 4.3
Mental preparation

Key terms

Anxiety The feeling of fear that we experience that something might go wrong either in the present or in the future.

Cognitive anxiety management techniques Those ways of coping that affect the mind and therefore can control anxiety.

Somatic anxiety management techniques Those ways of coping that affect the body directly such as relaxation. Cognitive can affect somatic and vice versa.

> **STUDY HINT**
> You may be asked to explain how mental preparation can lead to a more successful performance in physical activities and sport.

Mental preparation techniques

Mental preparation techniques are widely used by those who participate in physical activities as well as sportsmen and women to cope with high levels of cognitive and somatic **anxiety (cognitive and somatic anxiety management techniques)**.

- **Practical example**: Controlling the heart rate by relaxation methods before a hockey match can make the player feel more positive about performing (somatic). Positive thinking can, in turn, control our heart rate (cognitive).

The following stress management techniques can be used as coping strategies.

Imagery

Imagery can improve concentration. The creation of pictures in our minds is imagery. Many people try to get the feeling of movement or capture an emotional feeling, for example of pleasure or happiness.

Imagery can also help with relaxation. A participant in a physical activity or a performer in sport who feels anxious could go to 'another place' in their minds to try to calm down. Many participants report that they use these techniques to cope with stress and anxiety.

Mental rehearsal

Imagery as a tool for relaxation is a form of mental rehearsal. Mental rehearsal can involve both internal and external imagery:

- External imagery is when you can picture yourself from outside your body, like watching yourself on film. For example, a racing car driver may go through the route in their mind before the race.
- Internal imagery is when you imagine yourself doing the activity and can simulate the feelings of the activity, such as the bobsleigh example or a high-jump athlete visualising the whole activity of run-up, jump and landing.

Mental rehearsal and imagery can result in the following benefits:

- Speeds up your reactions to different situations.
- Enables you to concentrate and focus.

- Keeps you calm and helps to control your levels of arousal.
- Can prepare you to react in different ways depending on the opponent or changing circumstances.
- Encourages you to be motivated and positive in your outlook.

To be effective in using selective attention and imagery the following points should be taken into consideration:

- Relax in a comfortable, warm setting before you attempt to practise mental rehearsal or imagery.
- If you want to improve skill by using mental rehearsal or imagery, then practise in a real-life situation.
- Mental rehearsal and imagery exercises should be short but frequent.
- Set goals for each session, e.g. concentrate on imagining the feel of a tennis serve in one short session.
- Construct a programme for your training in mental rehearsal or imagery.
- Evaluate your programme at regular intervals.
- **Practical example**: A winter Olympic athlete who is responsible for steering the team's bobsleigh visualises or uses imagery to picture the track, with all its bends, twists and turns. He goes through the movements he has to perform when he pictures each aspect of the run in his mind. This is an example of mental rehearsal.

▲ Figure 4.3.1 Mental rehearsal and imagery can help in reacting quickly to different situations

Selective attention

When learning skills or performing skills in sport it is often difficult for the learner or performer to discriminate between information that is relevant and information that is unimportant in the execution of the skill. A beginner basketball player may pay too much attention to the ball and not watch the movement of the opponent he is supposed to be marking. A badminton player may be paying too much attention to the movement of opponents rather than the flight of the shuttle. It is therefore important that when learning or performing a skill that needs more concentration, the performer concentrates on what is relevant and ignores irrelevant distractions. This process is called selective attention.

A goalkeeper in football may receive information that is not required to save the shot. There may be crowd noise and movement; movement of other players and the shouting of opponents to try to distract. The more experienced the goalkeeper, the more likely it is that the will be able to select out and filter this information.

The more tired the player, the less likely for the performer to be able to selectively attend or to concentrate on important pieces of information. Factors that affect selective attention include:

- relevance – the goalkeeper may judge that the striker's foot is more relevant than the waving of the crowd
- expectation – the goalkeeper expects there to be a shot because of the striker's body position
- vividness – a fellow player's loud shout is more likely to be attended to than a passing comment from another.

Positive thinking

This technique, sometimes called 'self-talk' involves the participant in a physical activity or the sports performer being positive about past experiences and performances and future efforts by talking to themselves or thinking through how successful they might be. This technique has been shown to help with self-confidence and to raise levels of aspiration. Unfortunately, for many would-be participants in physical activities and performers in sport, thinking can be far from positive and often can be negative. It is very common for sports performers to 'talk themselves out of winning', for instance a penalty taker saying to herself, 'I will probably miss this'. It is also common for young people to say that they do not want to exercise because they feel they might look foolish or will be embarrassed in front of others. This is known as negative self-talk or negative thinking and should be minimised if people are to participate in physical activities or for sports performance to be good.

High-level performers cannot afford to be negative and they must develop strategies to change these negative thoughts into positive ones (for example by not concentrating on what would happen if they lose, rather what will happen when they win).

There are five categories of negative thoughts:

1. Worry about performance, e.g. 'I think she is better than me.'
2. Inability to make decisions, e.g. 'Shall I pass, shall I hold, shall I shoot?'
3. Preoccupation with physical feelings, e.g. 'I feel too tired, I'm going to give up and rest.'
4. Thinking about what will happen if they lose, e.g. 'What will my coach say when I lose this point?'
5. Thoughts of not having the ability to do well, e.g. 'I am not good enough; he is better than me.'

Activity

Read the adjacent negative statements again. Now change each statement into a positive one.

❓ Extend your knowledge

The following are examples of activities that help athletes to mentally prepare.

Relaxation

Somatic anxiety can lead to cognitive anxiety, so the more physically relaxed you can get, the more mentally relaxed you can get. There is of course a happy medium in physical activities – you do not want to be too laid back because you often need to react quickly and dynamically.

Relaxation exercises before you attempt to train yourself in mental exercises such as imagery can be very useful. It helps the sports person to be calmer and steadier before performance. Relaxation skills are like any other type of skill: you need to practise hard to achieve them.

Self-directed relaxation

Like other techniques, this needs practice to be effective. Each muscle group is relaxed one at a time and the coach can help. The athlete then practises without direct help. Eventually it will take only a very short time for full relaxation. This time factor is crucial if the athlete is to be able to use the strategy just before or during competition.

Progressive relaxation training (PRT)

This is sometimes referred to as the Jacobsen technique, named after its pioneer. The athlete learns to be aware of the tension in the muscles and then releases all that tension. Because the athlete is so aware of the tension in the first place, they have a more effective sense of losing it when it goes.

IN THE NEWS

An example of positive thinking and concentration

In the 2014 Commonwealth Games women's netball semi-final, England played New Zealand and lost by one point (35 points to 34). The New Zealand team showed more effective concentration in the final seconds of the game.

Asked whether she feared New Zealand might have blown it when England attacked with the scores tied in that final minute, the Kiwis' wing attack Liana Leota replied: 'No, I never thought that. I knew we had the patience and still enough opportunity. We practise for situations like that in our training, so we know what the pressure is going to be like, how to absorb it and what structures to put in place. We are prepared.'

▲ Figure 4.3.2 Positive thinking can help in team performance

SUMMARY

- Mental preparation techniques can help performers in sport in many different ways.
- Each technique can help them to focus, control their anxiety and motivate them to do well. Imagery can help in controlling your levels of anxiety before and during performance.
- Mental rehearsal and selective attention help with focus and concentration and also help the performer to block out irrelevant stimuli and to attend to relevant stimuli or information.
- As a result, reaction time can be shortened and performance improves.
- Positive thinking helps particularly with motivation and for the performer to stick to the task and to try to do their very best.

Practice questions

1. What is meant by imagery? Using a practical example, show why you might use selective attention when performing in sport. **(4 marks)**

2. Explain how you might use different mental preparation techniques to optimise performance in sport. **(6 marks)**

3. Which one of the following is an example of positive thinking in sports performance? **(1 mark)**
   a. A triple jump athlete going through each part of the movement in her mind
   b. A dancer concentrating on one part of the surrounding wall when doing a spin
   c. A hockey player asking the umpire whether a goal has been allowed
   d. A rugby player visualising winning the national tournament

Understanding the Specification

You should be able to understand different types of guidance, their advantages and disadvantages, and be able to apply practical examples to their use. The types of guidance that can be examined are:

- visual
- verbal
- manual
- mechanical.

You should also be able to understand different types of feedback and apply practical examples. The types of feedback that can be examined are:

- intrinsic
- extrinsic
- knowledge of performance
- knowledge of results
- positive
- negative.

Guidance and feedback that are effective will help the learning of sports skills. Guidance is often given before the activity, whereas feedback is given during or after.

Guidance

When a teacher or coach teaches a new skill to a student or seeks to develop the skills of an experienced performer, they need to decide the best way to transmit the knowledge necessary for effective performance. There are four main types of guidance:

- visual, e.g. a coach demonstrating a set shot in basketball
- verbal, e.g. a teacher telling a pupil to watch the ball when receiving a pass in rugby
- manual, e.g. a coach supporting a gymnast in a vault
- mechanical, e.g. a learner swimmer using armbands/a trampolinist using a harness.

▲ Figure 4.4.1 A harness in trampolining is an example of mechanical guidance

The type or combination of types chosen depends on the personality, motivation and ability of the performer, the situation in which learning or development of skills is taking place and the type of skill being taught or developed.

Visual guidance

Visual guidance is widely used when teaching motor or movement skills. During the early phase of skill learning, visual guidance (often a demonstration by the instructor or another competent performer) helps the learner develop a mental image of what needs to be done.

Some instructors use videos, charts or other visual aids to build up the 'ideal' picture of what is required to successfully perform a new skill. The demonstration must be accurate so that there is no possibility of the learner building up an incorrect picture. To avoid confusing the learner and overloading them with information in the early stages of learning, it is important to concentrate on only a few aspects of the skill. The teacher may therefore 'cue' the performer on only one or two aspects of the whole movement.

The following points should be considered before using visual guidance:

- Demonstrations must be accurate and should hold the performer's attention.
- Demonstrations must be repeated but should not be too time consuming.
- Videos can be useful, especially if they have a slow-motion facility, but the student must be able to copy the model presented.
- For a learner to gain maximum benefit, their position during training should be considered. For example, the demonstration of a swimming stroke is best viewed from above on the poolside.
- During the early phase of skill learning, visual guidance is important for the learner to develop a mental image of what needs to be done.

Advantages:

- Good for beginners because they can easily visualise the correct movement skill.
- Easier to remember and to form a technical model to copy.
- Quick and effective.

Disadvantages:

- If demonstrations are incorrect then the wrong movement patterns are learned.
- Difficult to get the feel or kinaesthetic sense of the skill.
- May be too complicated for effective understanding.

Verbal guidance

This is often associated with visual guidance, being used to describe the action and explain how to perform the activity. Verbal guidance has limitations if used on its own – motor skills are difficult to describe without a demonstration of some kind. Remember that the instructor is trying to create an image in the learner's mind of what needs to be done. Verbal guidance of the more advanced performer is effective when more information, such as tactics or positional play, needs to be given.

Activity

Choose a skill from any sport. How would you teach this skill with visual guidance only?

▲ Figure 4.4.2 Verbal guidance can be effective in giving information about positional play

When using verbal guidance the teacher/coach needs to be aware of the following points:

- Do not speak for too long – sports performers have notoriously short attention spans.
- Some movements simply cannot be explained – stick to visual guidance in these cases.
- Direct verbal guidance is better in the early stages to ensure that the learner has a clear idea of what needs to be done.
- Questioning techniques can encourage personal development and develop confidence if handled in the right way, especially for the more advanced performers.

Feedback from the performers will also test understanding.

Advantages:

- Can be given immediately and quickly.
- Good for fine tuning a skill or developing skilled movements.
- Can be motivating and can, along with visual, develop a better understanding of the skill.

Disadvantages:

- Might be the wrong information given.
- Can lead to misunderstanding/confusion.
- Cannot easily create a mental picture of movement requirements.

Manual and mechanical guidance

Manual guidance is giving physical support, often by the coach, whereas mechanical guidance involves using equipment to support and guide the performer. This involves two factors:

1. **Physical support for the performer by another person or a mechanical device**. This is commonly known as 'physical restriction'. An example of this is supporting a gymnast over a vault or the use of a twisting belt in trampolining.
2. **The response of the performer being directed physically by another person**. This is commonly known as 'forced response'. Holding the arms of a golfer and forcing their arms through the movement of a drive is an example of forced response.

139

Key term

Kinaesthetic sense This is the feeling or sense that we get through movement. Nerve receptors, called proprioceptors, found in muscles, ligament and joints, pick up signals that feed back to the brain to tell us where we are and what we are doing.

Advantages:

- Manual/mechanical guidance can reduce fear in dangerous situations. For instance, wearing armbands will help in learning how to swim.
- Can be much safer for the performer and therefore raise confidence levels.
- This method of guidance can give some idea of the feeling (kinaesthesis) of the movement.

Disadvantages:

- It could give unrealistic 'feeling' of the motion. For example, it is advisable to remove the armbands as soon as possible to be able to teach stroke technique in swimming.
- Performer becomes over-reliant on support and therefore does not learn to perform themselves.
- Can be dangerous if the mechanical guidance malfunctions or the physical guidance is weak or inappropriate.
- The **kinaesthetic sense** of cycling with stabilisers will be different to the feelings that you get from muscles when you are cycling without mechanical help. The same when you are learning to swim with armbands. Therefore, it is important to get the 'true' sense of the skill as quickly as you can in skill learning.

Feedback

Feedback can be given during the performance of a motor skill or after its completion or even during it. Feedback is most effective if it is given close to the performance so the performance is fresh in the participant's mind. Feedback motivates, changes performance or actually reinforces learning. The more precise the feedback, the more beneficial it is.

There are several forms of feedback:

- **Internal/intrinsic feedback**: this is a type of continuous feedback that comes from within the performer, for example the 'feel' of the skill.
- **External/extrinsic/augmented feedback**: feedback that comes from external sources, for example from sound or vision.
- **Knowledge of performance**: this is information about how well the movement is being executed, rather than the end result.
- **Knowledge of results**: this is a type of terminal feedback that gives the performer information about the end result of the response.
- **Positive feedback**: reinforces skill learning and gives information about a successful outcome.
- **Negative feedback**: information about an unsuccessful outcome, which can be used to build strategies that are more successful.

Application using practical examples:

- Intrinsic feedback, e.g. a swimmer diving off the blocks feels that their legs are straight.
- Extrinsic feedback, e.g. a hockey player sees the ball go into the net.
- Knowledge of performance – feedback about the quality of the performance, e.g. a coach informs a sprinter that their arms are in the correct position at 90 degrees.

- Knowledge of results – information relating to the end result, e.g. the goal keeper in football saves the penalty.
- Positive feedback, e.g. a teacher saying well done when a pass in netball is performed correctly/an ace is served in tennis.
- Negative feedback, e.g. a coach telling a badminton player that their grip is incorrect/doing a false start in swimming.

Two of these types of feedback are important for learning skills and sports performance:

- knowledge of results
- knowledge of performance.

Knowledge of results

This feedback is external and can come from the performer seeing the result of their response or from another person, usually a coach or teacher. It is extremely important for the performer to know what the result of their action has been. There can be very little learning without this type of feedback, especially in the early stages of skill acquisition.

Knowledge of performance

This is feedback about the pattern of movement that has taken, or is taking, place. It is normally associated with external feedback but can be gained through kinaesthetic awareness, especially if the performer is highly skilled and knows what a good performance feels like.

Both knowledge of results and knowledge of performance can help with a performer's motivation and therefore help to improve performance, but if used incorrectly they can also demotivate. If the movement and/or the result is good then the performer will feel satisfaction. Knowing that the movement and results are good will help the performer form a picture of what is correct and associate future successful performance with that picture, image or model.

External feedback should be used with care because the performer may come to depend too heavily upon it and will not develop internal feedback. The type of feedback that should be given depends on the ability of the performer, the type of activity being undertaken and the personality of the performer – different performers respond differently to different types of feedback. For any sort of feedback to be effective it needs to be accurate, understandable and given in a timely manner.

When performance is measured and this is given to performers as feedback, their motivation can be enhanced and their performance improved. Negative feedback can be used effectively at times as a motivational tool and to encourage self-reflection. Sports performers often set themselves targets from their previous performances, but teachers and coaches can help by constructing performance/goal charts that the performer updates as necessary. These charts serve as feedback on current performance and set clear and progressive targets (see goal setting).

? Extend your knowledge

Other types of feedback include:

- **continuous feedback:** feedback during the performance, either from the coach, instructor or teacher or from the continuous feel of the skill
- **terminal feedback:** feedback after the response has been completed.

STUDY HINT

It's important to be able to make the links between feedback and performance in sport. Make sure you're able to give relevant practical examples linking different types of feedback to improving performance in physical activities and sport.

SUMMARY

- There are four main types of guidance and six main types of feedback.
- Visual guidance is used in early stages of teaching a skill. Demonstrations are the most common form.
- Verbal guidance is not terribly effective if used on its own, except with very able performers.
- Manual and mechanical guidance are important in the early stages of learning. They can help a performer cope with fear and can help with safety.
- Feedback motivates, changes performance and actually reinforces learning.
- Both knowledge of results and knowledge of performance can help with a performer's motivation and therefore help to improve performance.
- For feedback to be effective it needs to be accurate, understandable and given in a timely manner.

Practice questions

1. Using practical examples, show how extrinsic feedback can be effective in sports performance. **(4 marks)**
2. Explain the advantages and disadvantages of manual and mechanical guidance. **(6 marks)**
3. Explain the uses of different types of feedback to motivate a sports performer and to ensure improved future performances in sport. **(10 marks)**

Section 5
Health, Fitness and
Well-being

5.1 Health, fitness and well-being
5.2 Diet and nutrition

Understanding the Specification

You should know what is meant by health, fitness and well-being and understand the different health benefits of physical activity (including physical, emotional and social aspects) and consequences of a sedentary lifestyle.

You should be able to apply the above to different age groups and respond to data about health, fitness and well-being.

Key term

Healthy lifestyle The World Health Organization (WHO) defines health as 'a state of complete physical, mental, and social well-being and not merely the absence of disease or infirmity'.

Healthy lifestyle

Many studies have revealed that a balanced, **healthy lifestyle** will help you to feel better and live longer. Taking exercise, not drinking too much alcohol, eating enough fruit and vegetables and not smoking can add up to 14 years to your life.

IN THE NEWS

Research involving 20,000 people over 10 years found those who did not follow a healthy lifestyle were four times more likely to have died than those who did. The findings held true regardless of how overweight or poor the people studied were.

The findings showed that it was in the reduction of deaths related to cardiovascular disease that people benefited most.

(Research by University of Cambridge and the Medical Research Council in the English county of Norfolk between 1993 and 2006.)

A healthy, balanced lifestyle means different things to different people and different cultures. Here in the UK there is general agreement that the following contribute to a healthy, balanced lifestyle:

- eating a healthy and balanced diet
- regular exercise – the current government recommendation is that adults should carry out a minimum of 30 minutes' moderate physical activity on five or more days a week, while children and young people aged 5–18 should participate in physical activity of moderate intensity for one hour a day
- maintaining a healthy body weight
- not smoking
- sensible alcohol consumption
- minimising stress.

An unhealthy lifestyle often includes the following:

- poor diet, e.g. excess fat, salt, sugar, protein and insufficient complex carbohydrate, vitamin/mineral and fluid intake

- inactivity and lack of exercise
- being overweight, which increases risk of certain types of cancers, high blood pressure, heart disease and diabetes
- smoking, which causes lung cancer, heart disease, chronic bronchitis, emphysema and is a risk factor for many cancers
- excess alcohol consumption, which increases risk of liver disease and mouth, throat and oesophageal (food pipe) cancer and can contribute to obesity
- high stress levels, whether associated with work, ineffective time management, or general lifestyle habits.

Fitness

The term **fitness** is often used loosely and frequently refers to aerobic endurance or how far you can run without getting too much out of breath. Fitness is more complex than that. It involves many different components or parts. Depending on the type of sport you are involved with you may be very fit in one component but not in another. For example, strength and power are very important to the discus thrower in athletics but less important in archery. All sports activities, however, require a good general level of fitness for all components. For some team games all components of fitness are equally important, although this may vary depending on what position you play. The following are recognised as the main components of physical fitness (more detail in Chapter 2.1):

- **Strength**: the ability of a muscle to exert force for a short period of time.

Key term

Fitness Usually related to physical fitness, this is a person's capacity to carry out life's activities without getting too tired. It is often used as a measure of the body's ability to function efficiently and effectively.

▲ Figure 5.1.1 Strength is the ability of a muscle to exert force for a short period of time

- **Muscular endurance**: the ability of the muscle or group of muscles to repeatedly contract or keep going without rest.
- **Aerobic endurance**: the ability to continuously exercise without getting tired.
- **Flexibility**: the amount or range of movement that you can have around a joint.
- **Power**: a combination of strength and speed, often referred to as fast strength.
- **Speed**: the ability of the body to move quickly.

▲ Figure 5.1.2 Speed is the ability of the body to move quickly

- **Body composition**: the way in which your body is made up.
- **Agility**: how quickly you can change direction under control.
- **Co-ordination**: ability to perform tasks in sport, for example running and then passing a ball in rugby.
- **Balance**: the ability to keep your body mass over a base of support, e.g. a gymnast performing a handstand on a balance beam.
- **Reaction time**: the time it takes someone to make a decision to move, e.g. how quickly a sprinter reacts to the gun and decides to drive off the blocks.

Well-being

Many people report that they feel better after participating in sport. It is accepted that certain hormones are released during exercise and that these can help us to feel more optimistic about life and better about ourselves. There is of course the additional benefit of meeting and participating with other people. New friends can be made through sport, which is an important factor in our sense of **well-being**.

An active lifestyle often includes the following benefits:

- Keeps the heart muscles in shape and makes the heart a more efficient pump.
- Increases blood flow and contributes to a reduction in risk factors for coronary heart disease.
- Reduces blood pressure, which is good because there is more stress on the arterial walls and this could cause a stroke or kidney failure.
- Reduces stress, which makes us feel better.
- Reduces diabetes risk, because an increase in body fat is often linked with type 2 diabetes.
- Increases 'good' cholesterol, which in this case is beneficial because 'good' cholesterol helps transport 'bad' cholesterol away and reduces the risk of heart disease.
- Promotes a feeling of well-being.
- Promotes a better social life/making friends.

Physical activity and sport can really help people to remain healthy and combat disease. A **sedentary** lifestyle (lack of physical activity) has many disadvantages and can cause mental and physical illness.

Key term

Well-being This refers to a feeling or mental state of being contented, happy, prosperous and healthy.

Key term

Sedentary This describes a lifestyle that is inactive and involves much sitting down. For example, if you worked on a computer all day in an office and then went home to sit and watch TV, your lifestyle could be described as sedentary.

▽ Table 5.1.1 A summary of the physical benefits from exercise and the consequences of a sedentary lifestyle

Factor (physical)	Benefit from exercise	Consequence of inactivity
Injury	Exercise will help injuries to heal and enable the body to retain its fitness levels – exercise could also cause injuries (see Chapter 2.3)	More likely to suffer stresses and strains through ordinary life activities because of the lack of physical fitness
Coronary heart disease (CHD)	Less likely to suffer from CHD. Exercise will help to keep the heart and blood supply healthy	Lack of exercise may cause CHD with poor blood and oxygen circulation and build-up of fat in the arteries
Blood pressure	More likely to be the normal levels for a healthy person	More likely to be raised, with health consequences (such as hypertension)
Bone density	More likely for bones to have normal bone density and be less likely to be damaged during everyday activities. During sport type exercise more risks for bones to be broken	Bone density not as healthy as an active individual with bones more likely to be weaker and more liable to damage
Obesity	Less likely for someone to be obese if regular exercise is a feature of their lifestyle. Exercise will ensure that energy taken in by the body is used well and less likely for fat deposits to be created around the body and its organs	More likely for the body's BMI to show too much body fat and therefore causing diseases such as CHD
Type 2 diabetes	This is less likely for those who exercise regularly with people having lower body fat and more normal blood sugar levels	This is more likely for those who are inactive. The body does not produce enough insulin and too much glucose remains in the blood. It is more associated with obesity and older people
Posture	Posture is more likely to be normal, with fewer problems with the muscles of the back. Activity can of course affect posture through injury	Poor posture can lead to muscle and skeletal damage and this is more associated with those who are inactive
Fitness	The more active you are, the much more likely you are to be fit and therefore have more energy for everyday life	If you are inactive you are more likely to be unfit and therefore will tire easily and be more likely to suffer from muscle damage

Emotional health benefits of physical activity and consequences of a sedentary lifestyle

▼ Table 5.1.2 The emotional health benefits of physical activity and the consequences of a sedentary lifestyle

Factor (emotional)	Benefit from exercise	Consequence of inactivity
Self-esteem/confidence	Exercise can help you feel better about yourself and feel confident in the way you look and that you can achieve fitness goals. Activity can help to release hormones that make you feel better and happier	Inactive people may well have low self-esteem because they lack energy but also because they are more likely to be obese, which can also be a contributory factor for low self-esteem
Stress management	An active person often feels that the stresses of everyday life can be forgotten or released through exercise and so they manage stress more effectively	When inactive a person may dwell on life's difficulties and may not have enough outlets to get rid of stress and anxiety
Image	An active person is more likely to have a good level of self-image. In other words, they feel that they look good to themselves and to others	Inactive people can have a poor self-image. This feeling of inadequacy can arise from poor body image, which can, in some cases, be related to obesity or sometimes those who are extremely underweight

Social health benefits of physical activity and consequences of a sedentary lifestyle

▼ Table 5.1.3 The social health benefits of physical activity and consequences of a sedentary lifestyle

Factor (social)	Benefit from exercise	Consequence of inactivity
Friendship	Exercise can help people make friends with others who are involved in physical activities. The improved levels of self-esteem may also help people to make friends with others	A sedentary lifestyle can result in a person not going out very much and not meeting people. Inactive people may also have lower levels of confidence
Belonging to a group	Exercise enables people to belong to a team or an exercise class or a jogging club, for example. There are many opportunities for the more active to join groups and gain a sense of belonging	Inactivity can result in isolation for an individual and therefore that person may not feel they are part of a community and they could become dispirited
Loneliness	Exercise gives many opportunities to meet and be with other participants. Sports teams often have friendship groups within them, but also a collective identity. Those in a team can feeling that they belong and therefore are less likely to be isolated	Inactivity can result in a lack of people to talk to and this social isolation can lead to loneliness

STUDY HINT

When preparing for the examination in this topic area, divide up physical, emotional and social aspects of health and show how health, fitness and well-being can affect each aspect.

Physical	Emotional	Social
Injury Coronary heart disease (CHD) Blood pressure Bone density Obesity Type 2 diabetes Posture Fitness	Self-esteem/confidence Stress management Image	Friendship Belonging to a group Loneliness

❓ Extend your knowledge

The indicators of health and well-being

- **Satisfaction with aspects of life.** How satisfied do we feel about our lives overall? This does not mean that you will feel deliriously happy about everything, but overall to be a healthy and balanced individual you need to be pretty satisfied with the way things are generally going.

- **Frequency of positive and negative feelings.** How often do you feel very positive about life around you and how often do you have negative thoughts? The more positive thoughts you have, the more healthy and balanced you are likely to be, both mentally and physically.

- **Frequency of feelings or activities that may have a positive or negative impact on well-being.** Some of the feelings that you have or activities that you are involved in may have a real impact on how you feel; others often do not. For example, if you regularly play sport you may feel excited and enjoy being with others; this has a positive impact on the way you feel. If you are taking illegal drugs or are consuming too much alcohol this may also make you feel good in the short term but may have a lasting negative impact on your health and well-being.

- **Access to green space.** Do you have places around you that give you a sense of space? Those who live in overcrowded conditions and do not have anywhere around them that is spacious and has vegetation may well feel less good about their lives, which may have a negative impact on their health and well-being.

- **Level of participation in other activities.** Those who are active in many different ways are often the happiest. This is not always the case, but usually if you have a variety of interests, you have a better view of yourself and others.

- **Positive mental health.** If you feel happy, optimistic about the future and useful then you are more likely to have positive mental health. Those who are more relaxed, feel interested in other people and deal with problems well are also said to have positive mental health.

Activity

Well-being: how do you feel?

Below are some statements about feelings and thoughts. Tick the statements that best describe your experience over the last two weeks.

- I've been feeling optimistic about the future.
- I've been feeling useful.
- I've been feeling relaxed.
- I've been feeling interested in other people.
- I've had energy to spare.
- I've been dealing with problems well.
- I've been thinking clearly.
- I've been feeling good about myself.
- I've been feeling close to other people.
- I've been feeling confident.
- I've been able to make up my own mind about things.
- I've been feeling loved.
- I've been interested in new things.
- I've been feeling cheerful.

Once you have thought about your responses, rate yourself out of 10 for how good you feel. Are there any areas above that you have little control over, and if so, what can you do?

SUMMARY

- Health is a state of complete physical, mental and social well-being and not merely the absence of disease or infirmity.
- Sedentary is a word to describe a lifestyle that is inactive and involves much sitting down.
- Well-being refers to a feeling or mental state of being contented, happy, prosperous and healthy.
- Fitness – usually related to physical fitness – is a person's capacity to carry out life's activities without getting too tired.

Practice questions

1. What is meant by each of the following terms? **(3 marks)**
   - Health
   - Fitness
   - Well-being
2. Describe the physical consequences of a sedentary lifestyle and how this might change with age. **(10 marks)**
3. Explain the emotional benefits of regular exercise. **(6 marks)**
4. Outline the social benefits of regular exercise. **(4 marks)**

Understanding the Specification

You should know the definition and components of a balanced diet, as well as understand the effect of diet and hydration on energy use in physical activity. You should be able to apply practical examples from physical activity and sport to diet and nutrition.

Diet and nutrition

The healthy diet

A **balanced diet** is a diet based on:

- starchy foods such as potatoes, bread, rice and pasta
- plenty of fruit and vegetables
- some protein-rich foods such as meat, fish and lentils
- some milk and dairy foods
- not too much fat, salt or sugar.

A balanced diet means eating a wide variety of foods in the right proportions and consuming the right amount of food and drink to achieve and maintain a healthy body weight.

The following are the main nutrients or essential components the body requires to follow an active, healthy lifestyle.

Carbohydrates

These are made up of the chemical elements of carbon, hydrogen and oxygen. Carbohydrates are primarily involved in energy production. There are two forms of carbohydrate:

- simple sugars – these provide a quick energy source and include glucose and fructose
- complex starches – these have many sugar units and are much slower in releasing energy.

Carbohydrates are very important to the athlete, especially in exercise that is highly intense. They are also essential to the nervous system and determine fat metabolism.

Key term

Balanced diet This involves taking the right amount or level of energy and nutrients that the body needs in its expenditure of energy. In other words you need to have the energy output balancing with energy input. A balanced diet for humans is one that contains the correct proportions of carbohydrates, fats, proteins, vitamins, minerals, and water necessary to maintain good health.

▲ Figure 5.2.1 Carbohydrates are very important to the athlete, especially in exercise that is highly intense

? Extend your knowledge

When exercise takes place, glycogen is broken down to glucose, which supplies muscles with energy. When glycogen stores are depleted, there is less energy available and the participant in exercise will become fatigued. If you are eating about 2,500 calories a day, the recommend ed daily intake of carbohydrate is at least 313 grams. For 2,000 calories it is at least 250 g, and for 1,500 calories it is 188 g.

Key terms

Saturated fats A saturated fat is in the form of a solid, e.g. lard, and is primarily from animal sources.

Unsaturated fats An unsaturated fat is in the form of liquid, e.g. vegetable oil, and comes from plant sources.

Carbohydrates are stored in the muscles and the liver as glycogen but in limited amounts that need to be replenished. Sources of carbohydrates include:

- complex – cereal, pasta, potatoes, bread, fruit
- simple – sugar, jam, confectionery, fruit juices.

It is recommended that about 60 per cent of an athlete's diet should consist of carbohydrates.

IN THE NEWS

Eating the right amount for your needs

Leading up to the Beijing Olympics in 2008, the gold medallist swimmer Michael Phelps was reported to have eaten about 12,000 calories per day. He needed this because of t.he tremendous amount of energy he required for training and competing.

Energy input must match energy output if you are to follow a balanced diet and not develop too much body fat or become underweight and therefore weaker.

Fats

These are a major source of energy for athletes performing low-intensity endurance exercise. They play an important role in insulating the body. Fats or lipids are made up of carbon, hydrogen and oxygen but in different proportions to carbohydrates. There are two types:

- triglycerides, which are stored in the form of body fat
- fatty acids, which are used mainly as fuel for energy production; these are either **saturated fats** or **unsaturated fats**.

When muscles' cells are readily supplied with oxygen, fat is the usual fuel for energy production. This is because the body is trying to save the limited stores of glycogen for high-intensity exercise and therefore delays the onset of fatigue. The body cannot solely use fat for energy and so the muscle is fuelled by a combination of fat and glycogen.

Fat consumption should be carefully monitored and can cause obesity. Fat is very important to protect vital organs and is crucial for cell production and the control of heat loss. It is generally accepted that a maximum of 3 per cent of total calories consumed should be from fatty foods. Examples of sources of fats:

- saturated fats – meat products, dairy products, cakes, confectionery
- unsaturated fats – oily fish, nuts, margarine, olive oil.

Obesity

The main measurement of obesity is the body mass index (BMI). This is your weight in kilograms divided by your height in metres squared. For example, someone who weighs 100 kilograms and is 1.8 metres tall has a BMI of

30.86 (100 divided by 3.25 [1.8 squared]). Individuals are defined as being overweight if their BMI is 25–29.9 and obese if their BMI is 30 or over. Obesity contributes to a range of problems, including heart disease, type 2 diabetes, osteoarthritis and some cancers. Experts say that obesity is as serious a health problem as smoking or excessive alcohol consumption.

Protein

Proteins are composed of carbon, hydrogen, oxygen and nitrogen and some contain minerals such as zinc. Proteins are known as the building blocks for body tissue and are essential for repair. They are also necessary for the production of haemoglobin, enzymes and hormones. Proteins are also potential sources of energy but are not used if fats and carbohydrates are in plentiful supply.

Protein should account for approximately 15 per cent of total calorie intake. If protein is taken excessively then there are some health risks, for example kidney damage due to excreting so many unused amino acids. Examples of sources of protein:

- Meat, fish and poultry are the three primary complete proteins.

Vegetables and grains are called incomplete proteins because they do not supply all the essential amino acids.

Protein breaks down more readily during and immediately after exercise. The amount of protein broken down depends upon how long and how hard you exercise. Increased protein intake may be important during the early stages of training to support increases in muscle mass and myoglobin.

The following nutrients are essential but needed in small quantities only and are often referred to as micronutrients.

Vitamins

Vitamins are non-caloric chemical compounds that are needed by the body in small quantities. They are an essential component of our diet because they are vital in the production of energy, the functioning of our metabolism and the prevention of disease. With the exception of vitamin D the body cannot produce vitamins. Vitamins A, D, E and K are fat-soluble. Vitamins B and C are water-soluble.

A well-balanced diet will ensure sufficient vitamin intake. Vitamins can be found in fresh fruit and vegetables.

Extremely large doses of vitamins can be dangerous. An overdose of vitamin A can cause hair loss and enlargement of the liver. There is little evidence to suggest that supplementary vitamin pills can enhance performance and most excess vitamins are simply excreted via urine.

Minerals

These are also non-caloric and are inorganic elements essential for our health and for chemical reactions in our body. There are two types:

- macro-minerals – needed in large amounts, e.g. calcium, potassium and sodium
- trace elements – needed in very small amounts, e.g. iron, zinc and manganese.

? Extend your knowledge

To make sure you get enough vitamins from your food:

- buy good-quality fresh fruit and vegetables
- wash/scrub food rather than peeling it because vitamins are often found just below the skin
- prepare just before cooking and boil for a short time and in as little water as possible; steaming or microwave cooking is even better
- eat soon after cooking.

Minerals can be lost through sweating and so there are implications for those who exercise. Minerals should be replaced quickly to ensure good health. Some important minerals are listed below.

Iron

This is an essential component of haemoglobin, which carries oxygen in the blood. Iron-deficiency anaemia can impair performance in endurance events.

IN THE NEWS

Research has shown that 36–82 per cent of female runners are anaemic and therefore should seek iron-rich foods in their diets. Only a qualified medical doctor should prescribe iron supplements because too much iron can be dangerous. Iron can be found in meat, fish, dairy produce and vegetables. Main sources are red meat and offal.

Calcium

This mineral is essential for healthy bones and teeth. If there is deficiency in calcium, then there is an increased likelihood of osteoporosis and bone fractures. For calcium to be absorbed, there needs to be sufficient vitamin D, which is found in sunlight.
Calcium is found in milk and dairy products, green vegetables and nuts.

Fibre

Fibre is essential to ensure a healthy, balanced diet. Fibre in foods is known as dietary fibre and is found in foods such as fruit and vegetables as well as cereals, beans, lentils and wholemeal bread.
For the digestive system to work effectively it is important to consume dietary fibre. For the large intestine to work properly and waste to be excreted effectively by the body, dietary fibre should part of your everyday diet. A high-fibre diet has also been shown to reduce cholesterol and to limit the risk of diabetes and obesity. The NHS advises that we consume about 18 grams of fibre per day. However, most do not reach this level.

Water and hydration

This is also a nutrient and is crucial for good health, particularly for those who participate in sport. It carries nutrients in the body and helps with the removal of waste products. It is also very important in the regulation of body temperature. The body loses water through urine and sweat. This water loss accelerates depending on the environment and the duration and intensity of any exercise.
On average individual daily consumption of water should be about two litres. Those involved in exercise should take more to ensure a good state of hydration. Studies show that individuals who are dehydrated become intolerant to exercise and heat stress. The cardiovascular system becomes inefficient if there is dehydration and there is an inability to provide adequate blood flow to the skin, which may lead to heat exhaustion.
Fluids must be taken in during prolonged exercise. This will minimise dehydration and slow the rise in body temperature.

? Extend your knowledge

Calcium deficiency

Calcium deficiency can be found in females who are underweight, smokers, alcoholics, vegans and those who overdo training and exercise.

There are a number of commercially available sports drinks containing electrolytes and carbohydrates. Some of the claims that are made about these drinks have been misinterpreted. A single meal, for instance, can replace the minerals lost during exercise. Water is the primary need in any drink taken before, during and after exercise because it empties from the stomach extremely quickly and reduces hydration associated with sweating. Thirst is not a reliable indicator for fluid intake; therefore it is best to drink small amounts regularly even if you are not thirsty. Under cooler conditions, a carbohydrate drink may give the extra energy needed in events or periods of exercise lasting over an hour.

Composition of a healthy diet

Healthy eating involves a daily calorie intake in approximately the following proportions:

- 50 per cent carbohydrate
- 30–35 per cent fat
- 15–20 per cent protein.

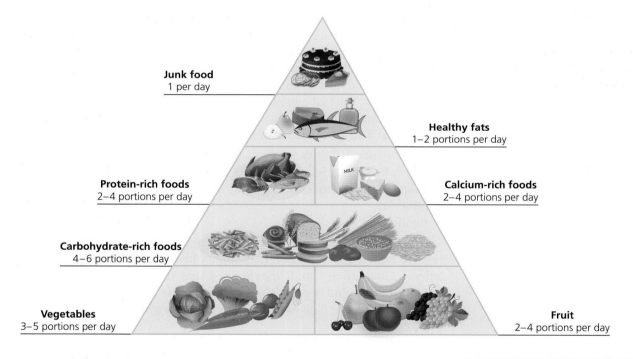

Junk food
1 per day

Healthy fats
1–2 portions per day

Protein-rich foods
2–4 portions per day

Calcium-rich foods
2–4 portions per day

Carbohydrate-rich foods
4–6 portions per day

Vegetables
3–5 portions per day

Fruit
2–4 portions per day

When planning your diet you should also take the following into consideration:

- Food is meant to be enjoyed.
- Avoid too much fat.
- Avoid too many sugary foods.
- Include vitamins and minerals.

❓ Extend your knowledge

Alcohol

Alcohol is a concentrated source of energy but cannot be available during exercise for our working muscles.

- Eat plenty of fibre.
- Keep alcohol within prescribed limits (for those over 18).
- Maintain balance of intake and output.
- Eat plenty of fruit and vegetables.

The Health Development Agency and the National Institute for Health and Clinical Excellence recommend the following as the maximum intake of alcohol for adults (over 18s):

- males – 3–4 units per day
- females – 2–3 units per day.

Most advisers agree that 'binge drinking', a growing habit among teenagers and young adults, is particularly bad for you. If you are of the legal age to drink it is better to spread your alcohol consumption across the week and to leave some alcohol-free days.

One unit:

- half pint 'ordinary strength' beer = 3.0–3.5 per cent alcohol = 90 calories
- 1 standard glass of wine = 11 per cent alcohol = 90 calories
- single measure spirits = 38 per cent alcohol = 50 calories.

There are no healthy or unhealthy foods, there are only bad uses of food. The right balance in a diet is essential for health and fitness. Enjoyment is an important aspect of eating; a healthy diet does not mean that you have to give up all your favourite 'bad' foods – it is the overall balance that counts. Balanced meals contain starchy foods with plenty of vegetables, salad and fruit. Your fat content should be kept to a minimum by using low-fat or lean ingredients.

Factors that also affect choice of foods include:

- culture, morals, ethics
- family influences
- peer-group influences
- lifestyle
- finance.

Eating sufficient fruit and vegetables is important for a healthy diet. It helps to reduce the likelihood of coronary heart disease and some cancers. Government guidelines suggest that you should eat at least five portions of fruit and vegetables each day. This is not a scientifically proven formula but it gives us useful guidance about roughly the right levels of intake.

Most healthy eating guidelines warn against eating too much salt. If your diet contains too much salt, this may lead to high blood pressure, which can cause heart and kidney disease.

NICE (National Institute for Health and Care Excellence) recommends eating a healthy diet, which means you and your family should:

- base your meals on starchy foods such as potatoes, bread, rice and pasta, choosing wholegrain where possible
- eat plenty of fibre-rich foods such as oats, beans, peas, lentils, grains, seeds, fruit and vegetables, as well as wholegrain bread, and brown rice and pasta
- eat at least five portions of a variety of fruit and vegetables a day in place of foods higher in fat and calories

---

? Extend your knowledge

What is a portion of fruit or vegetables?

- 2 tablespoons of vegetables
- 1 dessert bowlful of salad
- 1 apple/orange/banana
- 2 plums
- 1 cupful of grapes/cherries
- 2 tablespoons of fresh fruit salad
- 1 tablespoon dried fruit
- 1 glass fruit juice

- avoid foods containing a lot of fat and sugar, such as fried food, sweetened drinks, sweets and chocolate (some takeaways and 'fast' foods contain a lot of fat and sugar)
- eat breakfast
- watch the portion sizes of meals and snacks, and how often you are eating
- avoid taking in too many calories from alcohol.

Effective nutritional strategies for those who exercise regularly

Glycogen stores

Ensuring that the body has enough glycogen is crucial for optimum energy supply. One method of increasing the glycogen available is through glycogen 'loading', sometimes known as carb-loading. This process involves the sports person depleting their stores of glycogen by cutting down on carbohydrates and keeping to a diet of protein and fat for three days. Light training follows, with a high-carbohydrate diet for three days leading up to the event. This has been shown to significantly increase the stores of glycogen and helps to offset fatigue. When carb-loading the diet should consist mainly of foods like pasta, bread, rice and fruit. Generally a high-carbohydrate diet will ensure that glycogen will be replenished during exercise.

Other energy-giving strategies:

- Consume carbohydrates 2–4 hours before exercise.
- Consume a small amount of carbohydrates within the first half an hour of exercise to ensure refuelling of glycogen.
- Eat carbohydrates straight after exercise for up to two days to replenish stores.

Fluids

You may lose up to one litre of water per hour during endurance exercise; therefore rehydration is essential, especially if there are also hot environmental conditions. As we have discovered, thirst is not a good indicator of dehydration, therefore the athlete needs to drink plenty during and after exercise even if they don't feel thirsty.

▲ Figure 5.2.3 You may lose up to one litre of water per hour during endurance exercise; therefore rehydration is essential

- Take fluids, preferably water, before exercise to ensure full hydration.
- Take fluids continuously during exercise even if not thirsty.
- Small amounts often is best.
- Take fluids straight after exercise before alcohol is consumed.
- Some sports-specific drinks may be useful for high-intensity and long-duration exercise.

Vitamin and mineral supplements

There is an increase in the body's requirements for vitamins and minerals if regular, intensive exercise takes place. This means that the athlete will eat more food because of the need for more energy. This in itself will mean that the body is receiving more vitamins and minerals. As we have already seen, large quantities of extra vitamins and minerals can damage health. Supplementing the athlete's diet can be beneficial in certain circumstances.

> **❓ Extend your knowledge**
>
> **Supplements**
>
> (Please note that supplementation is best undertaken with medical supervision.)
> - Smokers should consider extra vitamin C.
> - If you are planning to become pregnant, it is recommended that you take folic acid.
> - If you are on a diet and consuming less than 1,200 calories per day, supplements in low doses have been found to be beneficial.
> - If you are vegan or vegetarian and your diet is therefore restricted, multi-vitamins and mineral supplements could be useful.

Factors to consider with sports performers and nutrition

Sports performers, especially at the top level, have certain aspects to their lifestyles that should be considered when planning nutritional intake:

- timing of meals to fit around training and events
- ensuring that there is balance in the diet
- ensuring adequate fluid intake
- ensuring adequate iron intake
- diet should be suitable for very high workload, depending on the activity
- psychological well-being – if an athlete is unhappy with the diet, then even if physiologically beneficial, it could negatively affect performance because of psychological pressure
- there should be a sharing of ideas between coach/dietician and performer to agree the best strategy, depending on an individual's needs and perceptions
- obsession with food is common with high-performance athletes and should be avoided.

SUMMARY

- A balanced diet involves matching the energy being expended with that being consumed.
- The main measurement of obesity is the body mass index (BMI).
- Water carries nutrients in the body and helps with the removal of waste products. It is also very important in the regulation of body temperature.
- Carbohydrates are primarily involved in energy production, fats are a major source of energy and insulating the body, proteins help to build body tissue and are essential for repair.
- Vitamins are an essential component of our diet because they are vital in the production of energy and the prevention of disease.
- Minerals are essential for our health and for chemical reactions in our body.
- One method of increasing the glycogen available is through glycogen 'loading', sometimes known as carb-loading.

✔ Check your understanding

1. What is the definition of a balanced diet?
2. What are the components of a balanced diet?
3. What is the function of each component and why is each so important for an athlete?
4. What is the effect of hydration?

Practice questions

1. What is meant by a balanced diet?   (2 marks)
2. Outline the components of a balanced diet.   (7 marks)
3. Outline the importance of carbohydrates as a nutrient for an athlete.   (4 marks)
4. Why is hydration important in a balanced diet? (3 marks)
5. What dietary advice would you give a games player when following an exercise programme?   (8 marks)

Glossary

Adrenaline – This is a hormone released from the adrenal glands and its major action is to prepare the body for 'fight or flight'.

Anaerobic – This is when the body is working without the presence of oxygen, for example lifting something quickly off the floor or doing an activity such as sprinting for a ball. This type of activity can be carried out only for a short amount of time because of the lack of oxygen and the build-up of lactic acid.

Anticipatory rise – This is the raising of the heart rate before exercise begins. It is caused through the release of adrenaline, which is a hormone.

Antigen – Substance that causes your immune system to produce antibodies that fight disease.

Anxiety – The feeling of fear that we experience that something might go wrong either in the present or in the future.

Articulating bones – These are the bones that move within a joint.

Axes of rotation – The centre around which something rotates.

Balanced diet – This involves taking the right amount or level of energy and nutrients that the body needs in its expenditure of energy. In other words you need to have the energy output balancing with energy input. A balanced diet for humans is one that contains the correct proportions of carbohydrates, fats, proteins, vitamins, minerals, and water necessary to maintain good health.

Ballistic stretching – This uses the momentum (a tendency for the body to keep moving) of a moving body or a limb in an attempt to force it beyond its normal range of motion. This is different from dynamic stretching, which involves controlled gradual stretching up to but not beyond the normal range of movement.

Blood viscosity – This refers to the thickness of the blood and how resistant the blood is to flow freely. The more viscous the blood, the more it resists free flow. The amount of plasma or water content of the blood affects the viscosity. Therefore to ensure fast blood flow the plasma level needs also to be high.

Breathing rate – Sometimes called the respiratory rate or ventilation rate, it is the frequency of breathing measured in breaths per minute. Normal breathing rate at rest is approximately 12 breaths per minute.

Cardiovascular – Cardio means heart, vascular means circulatory networks of the blood vessels.

Cognitive anxiety management techniques – Those ways of coping that affect the mind and therefore can control anxiety.

Cognitive skills – These are skills that involve the intellectual ability of the performer. These skills affect the perceptual process and help us to make sense of what is required in any given situation. They are essential if the performer is to make correct and effective decisions.

Commercialisation – This refers to the influence of commerce, trade or business on an industry (e.g. sport) to make a profit.

Co-ordination – This is the ability to perform tasks accurately in sport.

Deviance – This involves human behaviour that is against your society's norms and values. Behaviour of this kind is often against the law.

Epiglottis – The main function of this flap of tissue is to close over the windpipe (trachea) while you're eating, to prevent food entering your airways.

Etiquette – This is about the customs we observe surrounding the rules and regulations of the physical activity and also about what is socially acceptable in a particular culture. It involves a convention or an accepted way of behaving in a particular situation.

Fitness – Usually related to physical fitness, this is a person's capacity to carry out life's activities without getting too tired. It is often used as a measure of the body's ability to function efficiently and effectively.

Gamesmanship – The use of unethical, although often not illegal, methods to win or gain a serious advantage in a game or sport.

Haemoglobin – This is iron-rich protein and transports oxygen in the blood. The more concentrated the haemoglobin, the more oxygen can be carried. This concentration can be increased through endurance training.

Hazard – Something that has the potential to cause harm.

Healthy lifestyle – The World Health Organization (WHO) defines health as 'a state of complete physical, mental, and social well-being and not merely the absence of disease or infirmity'.

Hypertrophy – This term means that there is an increase in the size or the mass of an organ in the body or a muscle. Hypertrophy often occurs as a result of regular training or exercise.

Insertion – This is the end of the muscle attached to the bone that actively moves, e.g. the biceps insertion is on the radius.

Kinaesthetic sense – This is the feeling or sense that we get through movement. Nerve receptors, called proprioceptors, found in muscles, ligament and joints, pick up signals that feed back to the brain to tell us where we are and what we are doing.

Lactic acid – With the absence of oxygen, lactic acid is formed in the working muscles. Lactic acid causes muscle pain and often this leads us to stop or reduce the activity we are doing.

Mechanical advantage – Some levers (first class and second class) provide mechanical advantage. This means that they allow you to move a large output load with a smaller effort. Load and effort are forces and are measured in Newtons (N).

Mechanical advantage is calculated as follows:

Mechanical advantage = Load ÷ Effort

For example, where the load = 500 N and the effort = 100 N, the mechanical advantage would be:

500 N ÷ 100 N = 5

Meniscus cartilage – In the knee, these are areas of cartilage tissue that act like shock absorbers in the joint.

Metabolism – This involves the many continuous chemical processes inside the body that are essential for living, moving and growing. The number of kilojoules the body burns is regulated by the rate of metabolism.

Mitochondria – These are parts of each muscle cell and places where energy is produced – sometimes referred to as 'powerhouses' of muscle cells. Those who exercise regularly and participate in endurance activities such as long-distance cycling often have more mitochondria.

Motor skill – An action or task that has a target or goal and that requires voluntary body and/or limb movement to achieve this goal. There are two main ways of using the word 'skill':

a. To see skill as a specific task to be performed.

b. To view skill as describing the quality of a particular action, which might include how consistent the

performance is and how prepared the performer is to carry out the task.

Muscular endurance – This is the ability of the muscle or group of muscles to repeatedly contract or keep going without rest.

Myoglobin – This is related to haemoglobin and is found in muscle cells that transport oxygen to the mitochondria to provide energy. Those who are more active – especially those who exercise regularly for endurance events such as marathon running – have higher levels of myoglobin.

Origin – This is the end of the muscle attached to a bone that is stable, e.g. the scapula. The point of origin remains still when contraction occurs.

Osgood-Schlatter's disease – This is a common cause of knee pain in children and is linked to bone and muscle growth.

Osteoporosis – This is a disease in which bones become fragile and more likely to break. If not prevented or if left untreated, osteoporosis can progress painlessly until a bone breaks. These broken bones, also known as fractures, occur typically in the hip, spine and wrist.

Oxyhaemoglobin – Haemoglobin combines with oxygen in the lungs to form a bright red chemical called oxyhaemoglobin. When the blood gets to places where oxygen is being used up, oxyhaemoglobin releases the oxygen and turns back into haemoglobin.

Participation rates – This refers to the number of people within a group who are involved in sport compared with those who are not. For example, in a school the participation rates of girls in extra-curricular sport could be 30 per cent. In other words, three out of every ten girls in the school are regular members of a sports team or club.

Perception – A complex concept that involves interpretation of stimuli. Not all stimuli are perceived and what is perceived depends on experience and attention ability.

Personal protective equipment – PPE (including correct clothing and footwear) is defined by the government's Health and Safety Executive as 'all equipment (including clothing affording protection against the weather) which is intended to be worn or held by a person at work and which protects him (or her) against one or more risks to his health or safety'.

Power – This is a combination of strength and speed.

Reaction time – This is the time it takes for you to initiate an action or movement, or the time it takes someone to make a decision to move, for example how quickly a sprinter reacts to the gun and decides to drive off the blocks.

Risk – The chance that someone will be harmed by the hazard.

Risk assessment – This is the technique by which you measure the chances of an accident happening, anticipate what the consequences would be and plan actions to prevent it.

Saturated and unsaturated fats – A saturated fat is in the form of a solid, e.g. lard, and is primarily from animal sources. An unsaturated fat is in the form of liquid, e.g. vegetable oil, and comes from plant sources.

Sedentary – This describes a lifestyle that is inactive and involves much sitting down. For example, if you worked on a computer all day in an office and then went home to sit and watch TV, your lifestyle could be described as sedentary.

Slow twitch fibres – (sometimes called type 1 muscle fibres) These are muscle fibres that can produce energy over a long period of time. They have high levels of myoglobin and mitochondria and are used for mainly aerobic activities.

Somatic anxiety management techniques – Those ways of coping that affect the body directly such as relaxation. Cognitive can affect somatic and vice versa.

Sport – This involves organised competition between individuals or teams that includes physical activity.

Sport England – Previously known as the English Sports Council, this organisation tries to help communities develop sporting habits for life. It funds other organisations and projects to get people more involved in sport and to help those who wish to pursue sport to the highest level.

Sportsmanship – This involves behaviour that shows fair play, respect for opponents and gracious behaviour, whether winning or losing.

Synovial joint – This is a freely movable joint in which the bones' surfaces are covered by cartilage, called articular cartilage, and connected by a fibrous connective tissue capsule (joint capsule) lined with synovial fluid.

Tendons – Muscles are attached to bones by tendons. These tendons help to 'pull' the muscle to the bone and help with the power of muscle contractions. Tendons are attached to the periosteum (a membrane that covers the outer surface of bones) of the bone through tough tissue called Sharpey's fibres.

Trachea – This is sometimes called the windpipe. It has 18 rings of cartilage, which are lined with a mucous membrane and ciliated cells, which trap dust. The trachea goes from the larynx to the primary bronchi.

Vascular shunt – This involves two processes:

- The arterioles (smaller arteries) experience vasodilation (diameter increases) and this increases the blood flow. Vasoconstriction (diameter decreases) of the arterioles that supply other organs such as the liver means that blood flow is lessened to these organs that do not require as much blood supply.

- In the capillaries that supply the skeletal muscles the precapillary sphincters (valves) open up and blood flow is again increased. In the capillaries that supply other organs, the precapillary sphincters close, thus decreasing the blood flow.

The result of these processes is to significantly increase the supply of oxygen to the working muscles during exercise.

Vasoconstriction – This occurs when the artery walls decrease their diameter.

Vasodilation – This occurs when the artery walls increase their diameter.

VO_2 max – The maximum amount of oxygen an individual can take in and use in one minute.

Well-being – This refers to a feeling or mental state of being contented, happy, prosperous and healthy.

Index